BARBECUE

This!

T0290227

BARBECUE This!

GET MORE OUT OF YOUR BBQ WITH 80 Delicious NEW RECIPES

LUKE HINES

plum. Pan Macmillan Australia

This book is dedicated to those willing to be the custodians of their own health and happiness through cooking with real food that's good for you and tastes great. Clink those tongs and have an absolute ball cooking from this book.

CONTENTS

INTRODUCTION

In all of my cookbooks I've celebrated one core principle that you'll see on each and every page and taste in each and every mouthful – it's gotta be real! And from day one my mission has been clear: celebrate real food in a way that respects your health and retains the integrity of every ingredient you use. I also believe that each meal you create should be easy, look fantastic and taste incredible. Flavour should never be compromised when looking after your health, which is why I love doing what I do – showing people that healthy food is delicious food.

Barbecue food, then, is a true representation of what I am about. It doesn't get any more real than cooking outdoors on an open flame, where there is no need to complicate things or trick anything up. It is about honest, simple cooking that celebrates the produce, adds incredible texture and delivers a depth of flavour to food that cannot be found elsewhere.

The barbecue is an iconic and timeless representation of our early beginnings. Thousands of years ago, our hunter–gatherer ancestors used fire for safety, survival, warmth, cooking and comfort, and here we are now in the modern day, still using it for the same reasons (albeit in a more convenient shape). For many years, I've believed in looking to our roots when it comes to nutrition by choosing unrefined and unprocessed ingredients and preparing them in a way that reflects the best modern learnings to help us thrive. So it's very synergistic that – after so many years of talking about the paleo and primal way of cooking and eating – this book celebrates cooking outside over an open flame.

The flames of a barbecue bring people together, connecting communities and providing a place of warmth and comfort. The barbecue has no borders and doesn't discriminate between race or cultures – across the globe it is a place for people to come together, to feed their family and friends, to help celebrate life events. And there is no doubt that, here in Australia, it holds a particularly special place in the hearts of so many. This book aims to amplify this love of being in our backyards, local parks or down the beach connecting, while also encouraging you to cook in a way that you might never have done before!

The human element of barbecuing is undeniable, but what it does to food is next level. The barbecue brings food alive and awakens all of the senses. There is the unmistakeable smell of the smoke, the extreme level of heat that can only be produced by a barbie and, of course, the resulting finish it gives food. From mouth-wateringly charred and crispy to sensationally smoky and succulent, the barbecue produces really special food with ease. It doesn't matter if it is fresh veggies and fruits or well-sourced, ethically raised animal proteins – you can cook close to anything on a barbecue!

And don't worry, I am not here to complicate your life with this book! You'll just need a barbecue that gives you plenty of controllable heat, the option to cook on a flat plate or grill and, for some recipes, the ability to cover and close the lid. This is not about complicating mealtimes – I am here to make things simple for you. I cover all the equipment you'll need and explain the different cooking methods over the following pages. So don't fret if you're new to all of this, I've got your back. You'll be a grill master in no time!

I've also created this book to prove that barbecuing is for everyone. Whether you follow a paleo, keto, low-carb, vegan, vegetarian or pescetarian way of eating – or just love barbecuing – this book is for you! And because my passion and qualifications are in health and nutrition, the food here is incredibly good for you – it is all made from scratch using the very best nutrient-dense ingredients. The food also follows the same ethos as my previous cookbooks, being completely free of grains, legumes, gluten and refined sugar. It's also very easy to make everything in this book dairy free, simply by replacing butter with extra-virgin olive oil. As always, I've tried to include plenty of plant-based options to fill your plates with colour, vibrancy and goodness. The salads chapter will have you eating the rainbow, the vegetable recipes are some of my all-time favourites, while the animal proteins span a wide variety of different cuts and celebrate family-friendly ingredients from cuisines all across the globe.

More than anything, though, I hope you find joy in the act of cooking real food from this book. Whether you're cooking for a housemate on your balcony, hosting a backyard gathering with the family, enjoying a beachside feast or camping, it's time to celebrate stepping outside of the kitchen and cooking some incredibly delicious food on the barbie!

x Luke Hines

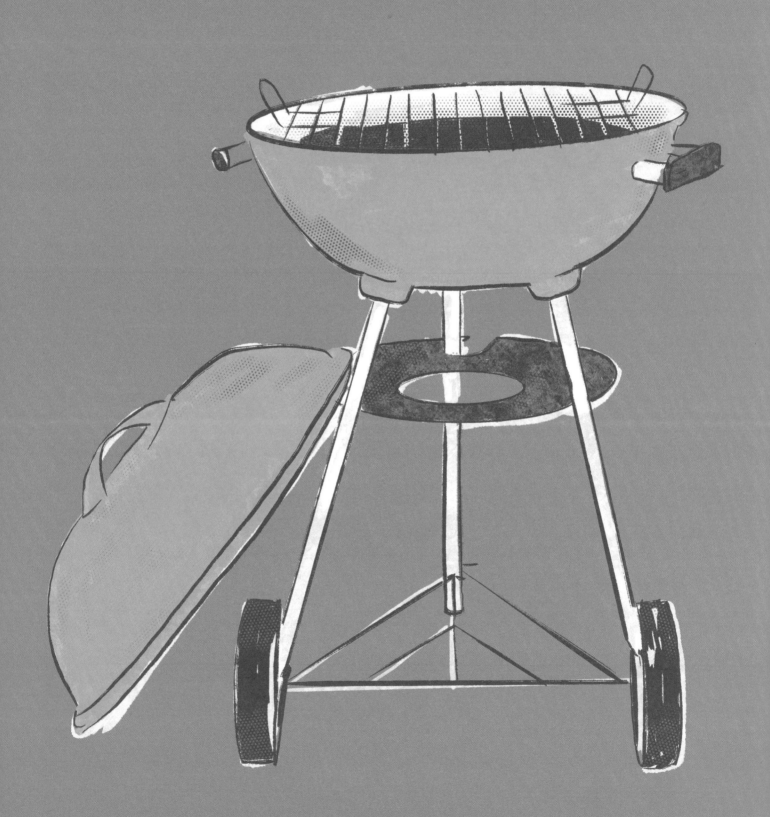

BARBECUE
basics

Whether you're just starting out or you've been barbecuing for years, for the most delicious results every single time you hit the hot plate, it's best to brush up on the basics. Here's where you'll learn which barbecue suits you best, how to bring it up to heat, the three key cooking methods and the tools that will come in handy.

CHOOSE YOUR BARBECUE!

There are so many different barbecues available, but to keep things simple I've written these recipes with the two most popular styles in Australia in mind – the everyday hooded gas barbecue and the charcoal-fuelled kettle style of barbecue. Both have the elements necessary for delivering the three key cooking methods used throughout the book – a flat hot plate (flat plate), a grill and a good solid lid to close. While the heat sources may differ in the ways detailed below, they both provide the cooking capabilities to make the most of this cookbook, so use what you've already got or choose whichever barbecue you think will work for the space and time you have and the type of food you want to cook.

GAS BARBECUES

- Short preheating time of 10–15 minutes.
- Very easy to control the heat and flames.
- Time efficient and convenient.
- Burns slightly cooler than charcoal.
- Exceptional sear on ingredients.
- Lighting is as simple as lifting the lid, turning on the gas and lighting the burners.
- Very easy to clean.
- A small metal 'smoker box' containing wood chips may be used on a gas grill to give a smoky flavour to the food.

CHARCOAL BARBECUES

- Involves building a fire of burning coals and sustaining it at the right level of heat for what you're cooking.
- Briquettes are the most common fuel source. (I recommend using pure hardwood ones that are all natural.)
- Charcoal can burn much hotter than gas, adding a smokiness and distinct flavour to the food.
- Predictable, even heat over a long period.
- 80–100 briquettes will last for about 1 hour.
- Be mindful to burn off any lighter fluid before you start cooking.
- Temperature of your charcoal fire will depend on how much charcoal you use and how long it's been burning.
- Coals are hottest when newly lit and lose heat over time.
- Once you've arranged your coals on the charcoal grate, place the lid on the grill and wait for 10 minutes for the temperature to rise to about 250°C. It'll preheat the cooking grate and make it easier to clean, and also create a better sear on your food.
- Can use wood chips for smoking. (Purists believe a charcoal barbecue is the only way to smoke.)

PREPARING YOUR BARBECUE FOR COOKING

Regardless of what type of barbecue you're cooking on, once it is preheated you'll want to clean the grate for a lovely, smooth cooking surface. Simply scrape off any residue with a long-handled grill brush. Unless specified in a recipe, oil the food not the barbecue to avoid any flare-ups and minimise wasted oil. If you do need to grease the grill, the best way to do this is to coat some paper towel with olive oil, then use either your hands or a pair of tongs to rub the paper towel over the grill or flat plate.

Preheating is a huge part of successful barbecue cooking, but so is being organised. While your barbecue is preheating, bring out all the ingredients and supplies you'll need (this will prevent you from having to run back inside later), and have everything chopped and measured beforehand. Take a look at my recommended equipment list on page 18 so you're good to go. And how many times have you cooked something delicious and had nowhere to put it? Always have some clean plates and platters by your side ready to transfer the cooked food to.

CHOOSE YOUR COOKING METHOD!

Now that we have covered different types of barbecues, let's delve deeper into the three main cooking methods used in this book and how they work. As I've already mentioned, both gas and charcoal barbecues support these methods, they just source the heat in slightly different ways. So, when cooking your food, take note of how to adjust the temperature of your barbecue for the best results.

FLAT PLATE
- A strong, solid cooking plate.
- Usually square or rectangular on a gas barbecue.
- Often an accessory or add-on for a charcoal barbecue.
- Provides a flat, even surface that conducts heat.
- Great for avoiding any flame flare-ups.
- Fantastic for cooking items that might fall through the cracks of a standard grill.

GRILL
- A strong cooking area of bars over the heat.
- Usually square or rectangular on a gas barbecue.
- The standard cooking style on a charcoal barbecue.
- Provides heat through the bars and from the flames in the gaps.
- Great for getting a flame-grill on food.
- Fantastic for cooking items that benefit from charring.

LID ON (CONVECTION)
- Uses a lid (which usually comes with a built-in temperature gauge) to contain the heat.
- Great for slow cooking.
- Great for keeping things warm.
- Great for containing and controlling your heat source.

SYMBOL KEY

You'll notice that most of the recipes in this book have a symbol up the top to show which cooking method they use as a quick and easy reference.

DIRECT VS INDIRECT HEAT

There are two main types of heat you can use when cooking on a barbecue – direct and indirect. By adjusting your heat source, you'll be able to achieve different results.

DIRECT COOKING

- Involves exposing food directly to the heat source.
- Most common with the flat plate or grill.
- Fastest way of cooking.
- Provides sear, char and flame.

INDIRECT COOKING

- Uses heat transfer like an oven.
- Usually paired with a closed lid for convection.
- Can be used with either grill or flat plate.
- The heat source is set away from the food.
- Good for slow cooking tougher cuts of meat or larger whole veggies.

To prepare a gas barbecue for cooking over direct heat, leave all of the burners on and adjust them to the heat level you want. To prepare it for indirect cooking, leave some of the burners on and turn one or two of them off. To prepare a charcoal barbecue for direct heat, simply spread the coals out over the whole area. To create a two-zone fire, spread the coals out on one side of the charcoal grate and leave the other side with no coals, so that you can cook over both direct and indirect heat.

GET YOUR TOOLS READY!

Let's talk good news first: I am here to tell you that you won't need any specialised equipment to whip up the dishes in this book. Don't get me wrong, if you want some super fancy rotisserie that turns your meat and bastes it for you, go right ahead! But the recipes to come are all quick and easy, super flavoursome and, above all, no fuss. Here are the basic tools that you'll need to get grilling.

FUEL
Full gas bottle or charcoal and/or briquettes, depending on what type of barbecue you are using.

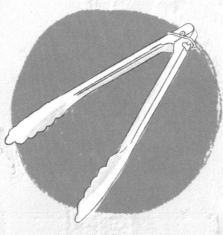

TONGS
Durable, spring-loaded and long enough to protect your hands and arms from the heat.

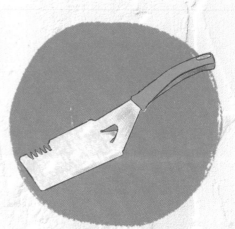

METAL SPATULA
Long handled and stainless steel, with a sharp cutting edge and front for ease of flipping food.

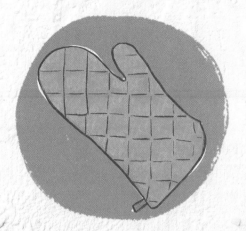

OVEN OR BARBECUE MITTS

For preparing your charcoal barbecue and handling hot utensils and equipment.

PAPER TOWEL

For unexpected spills and leaks, and to oil the grill or flat plate.

BASTING BRUSH

Choose one with bristles made from heat-resistant silicone that you can use for oils, bastes and sauces, and with a long handle to keep yourself a safe distance from the heat.

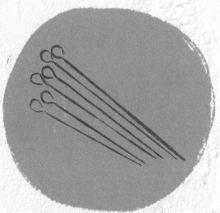

SKEWERS

Wooden, bamboo or metal will do (and lots of my recipes use them). Just be sure to soak your wooden and bamboo ones in cold water before use so they don't catch on fire!

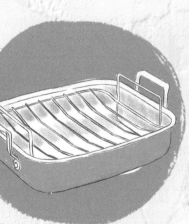
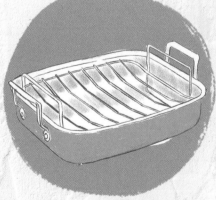

ROASTING TRAY

A large, heavy-based cast-iron roasting tray is perfect for convection-style cooking for slow-cooked recipes.

STEEL BRUSH

Solid and long handled, with securely anchored stainless-steel bristles for cleaning the barbecue before use. Choose one that can withstand a fair bit of pressure so you can get your elbow into it.

HOW TO USE THIS BOOK

I really want you to get the most out of this book, so here are the two ways you can best use all of the great information in here.

First off, the no-brainer is that you can simply select your favourite recipes from the chapters ahead, cook up an absolute storm and enjoy the rewards. Please be creative and give new types of recipes a go – you'll be amazed not just by how easy they are, but also how tasty each one of them is.

The second way you can use this book is to choose your meat, learn the heat and cook to perfection. To help you do this, I've created a guide on the following spread for different types of protein as well as fruit, showing recommended thickness, cooking time, heat and method – whether it's direct or indirect heat, flat plate, grill or closed-lid convection cooking.

And don't think I have forgotten flavour! Remember, I am all about seasoning like you mean it, so I've made a list all of the spice rubs, marinades, sauces and sides to help you get creative (see pages 25–27). You might want to pair my butter chicken spice rub with a whole chook instead of the skewers, or perhaps use the Middle Eastern marinade for lamb instead of beef. The choice is yours, so just follow the info on the coming pages and you'll soon be the master of your own grill.

CHOOSE YOUR MEAT, LEARN THE HEAT AND COOK TO PERFECTION!

Here is the lowdown on the best thickness, cooking time, method and heat for seafood, chicken, meat and fruit. Follow these simple guidelines and you'll have perfectly cooked food every single time you fire up the barbie.

FISH AND SEAFOOD

1. Fish fillet · 2.5 cm thick · Direct high heat · 8–10 minutes
2. Whole fish · 1 kg · Indirect medium heat · 20–30 minutes
3. Scallops · 50 g · Direct high heat · 2–4 minutes
4. Prawns · 50 g · Direct high heat · 2–4 minutes

CHICKEN

1. Chicken breast (boneless) · 200 g · Direct medium heat · 8–12 minutes
2. Chicken thigh (boneless) · 120 g · Direct medium heat · 8–10 minutes
3. Chicken mince burgers · 2.5 cm thick · Direct medium heat · 12–14 minutes
4. Whole chicken · 2 kg · Indirect medium heat · 1½ hours

PORK

1. Pork chop · 2.5 cm thick · Direct medium heat · 8–10 minutes
2. Pork mince burgers · 2.5 cm thick · Direct medium heat · 10–12 minutes
3. Pork tenderloin · 500 g · Direct medium heat · 15–20 minutes
4. Pork roast (boneless) · 1.5 kg · Sear then indirect high heat · 30–40 minutes

LAMB

1. Lamb chop · 2.5 cm thick · Direct high heat · 6–8 minutes
2. Lamb mince burgers · 2.5 cm thick · Direct medium–high heat · 8–10 minutes
3. Leg of lamb (butterflied) · 1.5 kg · Indirect medium heat · 30–45 minutes
4. Rack of lamb · 500 g · Sear then indirect medium heat · 15–20 minutes

BEEF

1. Beef steak · 2.5 cm thick · Direct high heat · 6–8 minutes
2. Beef mince burgers · 2.5 cm thick · Direct medium–high heat · 8–10 minutes
3. Beef kebab · 2.5 cm cubes · Direct high heat · 4–6 minutes
4. Rib roast (boneless) · 2.2 kg · Sear then indirect medium heat · 1½ hours

FRUIT

1. Apple · 1.25 cm thick slices · Direct medium heat · 4–6 minutes
2. Banana · Halved lengthways · Direct medium heat · 3–5 minutes
3. Peach · Halved lengthways · Direct medium heat · 6–8 minutes
4. Pineapple · 2.5 cm wedges · Direct medium heat · 5–10 minutes

CHOOSE YOUR FLAVOUR!

When it comes to barbecuing, you can get as creative as you like. Mix and match a spice rub or marinade to your favourite protein or veg, choose a sauce to drizzle over the top or a zingy salsa or dip to serve on the side. Here is a handy list of all the spice rubs, marinades, flavoured butters, sauces, dips, dressings, salsas and salads that appear throughout the book so you can mix and match to your heart's content.

In terms of what type of container you should use to marinate your meat or veggies in, your best bets are glass, stainless steel or ceramic bowls. There is no risk of corrosion with these materials, as opposed to aluminium or cast iron, which may react with acidic ingredients. Ziplock plastic bags are excellent for marinating, as are plastic containers, though there is some risk of staining with these materials and some acidic marinades can cause leaching over long periods of time. With all that in mind, glass is my top pick!

DRESSINGS

FLAVOURED BUTTERS

MARINADES AND FLAVOURED OILS

LUKE'S TOP 10 BARBECUE RULES

1. DON'T START COLD

Gas barbecues need about 10–15 minutes on high to preheat. Once hot, turn the heat down a little and heat for a further 10 minutes or so for medium–hot. For medium–low, reduce the heat a little more and heat for another 10 minutes. If you can, it's great to have one side on high and one side graduating down to low to slow things down while cooking if need be. Charcoal barbies need a little more care. Take the time to build the fire up and let it burn down for 30–40 minutes, and remember that you need to add a steady stream of fuel during cooking to keep it at temperature.

2. DON'T START DIRTY

A hot, clean barbecue will brown food better, with less chance of sticking. Your preheat time burns off any excess fat and dirt from the grill, flat plate and burners, giving your barbecue a good clean before cooking. Get stuck in there yourself as well using the strong brush recommended in the equipment list (see page 19), because a clean barbecue equals a successful meal.

3. SEASON LIKE YOU MEAN IT

Salt is your new best friend – nothing brings out flavour in barbecued food more – so find a great pink, rock or sea salt and keep it on hand. Extra-virgin olive oil and herbs are also your go-to for seasoning. Oiling your food first, then seasoning with your salt, herbs and spices helps them to stick on, while also reducing the chance of your food sticking to the barbecue.

4. MATCH MEAT TO HEAT

There is no one-size-fits-all approach when it comes to the right barbecue heat – you need to match the heat to your meat (or vegetables!). Usually, smaller, leaner cuts of meat require fast cooking over high temperatures, whereas thicker, fattier cuts of meat are best over low and slow heat. This is why having multiple heat zones on your barbecue is great for cooking the perfect dish. Create some direct and indirect heat zones and you'll be setting yourself up for barbecue success every time. And see page 22 for my handy guide to cooking different cuts of meat.

5. DON'T CROWD

Your barbecue is not the local Bunnings sausage sizzle, so please don't crowd the grill and flat plate like you're needing to feed the entire country. Always leave about one-quarter of your cooking space empty so that what you are cooking has space to breathe, there is room for your tongs and spatula to get in and around food, and you can adjust the heat zones appropriately.

6. LESS IS MORE

Leave your food alone! Don't stand there prodding and poking at it more than you need to. When you over-pierce and keep moving things around, you release all the juicy goodness, lose flavour and sacrifice those perfect char marks. Turn your ingredients only once or twice. If in doubt, wait it out, legends!

7. REST BABY REST

I can't stress enough how important it is to rest your protein after you've cooked it and removed it from the heat. Residual heat continues the cooking process once off the barbecue, giving your meat the best result. Plus, it allows all the juices to relax and settle in the protein, meaning that when you cut into your meat they don't just drain out all over the plate, leaving your dish bland and dry. My recipes specify the perfect resting time depending on what you're cooking.

8. BE CREATIVE

I understand we all get into the routine of cooking the same types of meals over and over. It's safe and feels comfortable because you know what you're doing. But this book is designed to get you away from simple snags and steak. Give yourself the challenge of trying a new recipe from each chapter every time you open your grill – you'll thank me later and they'll soon become staples that you can whip up anytime.

9. PERFECT PAIRINGS

Most of my animal protein recipes come with just a simple sauce or side, meaning you'll have time to make one of the incredible salad or veg recipes in here, too! You'll see lots of my recipes include some great main, side and salad pairing suggestions, so don't forget to hero all the ingredients at the barbecue – yup, meat AND veg!

10. KEEP A LID ON IT

When a recipe says to close the lid of the barbie for convection-style cooking, I suggest you keep it shut for the recommended time. This will maintain an even cooking temperature, make sure your food actually cooks through and help control flare-ups, as well as capturing that incredible smokiness that only barbecuing can create.

ON A SERIOUS NOTE

With every book I write I am passionate about sharing my love for real food and my ethos for health and happiness – for ourselves and also for the sustainability of our environment, farming practices and the food chain.

Every time you purchase food it is a chance for you to vote with your dollar. A vote that can support farms, producers and companies that do the right thing. If we support those who are doing the right thing, we enable them to continue to thrive, gain more awareness and lower the cost for everyone to be a part of that food chain.

The environment counts. We can't spend our time on this earth making decisions without thinking about the consequences of the footprint we are leaving for future generations. So look to support those who use holistic and regenerative farming practices, so that we know we will have food security for the future.

Crap food equals a crap life. There is no gentle way of saying it, really. When we fill our bodies with junk, we feel like junk, and we make decisions from a place not conducive to health and happiness. Fuel your body with the good stuff and you'll be feeling so good that you approach your life with positivity.

Please choose free-range poultry and eggs, grass-fed beef and butter, sustainable line-caught seafood and free-range nitrate-free pork. If your budget permits, take the next step and choose the organic versions of these. A healthy, happy animal, eating a diet it was designed to eat and then killed humanely, results in the best and most nutritious protein.

When it comes to fruit and vegetables, please start by shopping local, reducing your food miles and supporting local farmers. By buying fruits and veggies that are in season you support crops growing in natural circumstances. If your budget permits, please also choose organic, where possible, to reduce any potential herbicides or pesticides creeping into your system and to support sustainable farming practices.

When choosing sauces and dressings, if you're not making your own, please choose low-sugar varieties, sweetened with stevia, maple syrup or monk fruit syrup. If you're buying store-bought pesto, dip, mayo and aioli, please look for ones made with olive oil, and avoid those with highly refined hydrogenated seed oils, such as vegetable, canola or sunflower oil, which can increase inflammation. If in doubt, stick to what our grandparents cooked with – all the real, unrefined ingredients, such as extra-virgin olive oil, butter, ghee, tallow, lard and duck fat.

And, finally, always cook from a place of love. How you're feeling during the cooking process is always reflected on the plate. Whether it is stress or a feeling of being rushed or frazzled, it lands on the plate whether you want it to or not. So cook with care, calm and clarity, and you'll sit down to a meal that is truly good for you, inside and out.

Happy cooking, friends!

VERY good VEG

The crazy flavours from this combination of ingredients are truly something special, and will have your guests wowed before the main course has even arrived. I really believe you've not had butter until you've tried this anchovy butter, which also makes the most incredible addition to my steaks on pages 164, 168 and 172.

CHARRED ASPARAGUS
with ANCHOVY BUTTER

2 bunches of thick asparagus,
ends trimmed
2 tablespoons extra-virgin
olive oil
sea salt and freshly ground
black pepper
½ teaspoon chilli flakes

ANCHOVY BUTTER

125 g unsalted butter, softened
4 garlic cloves, crushed
8 anchovies in oil, drained and
finely chopped
½ teaspoon hot paprika
½ teaspoon lemon juice
sea salt, to taste
1 tablespoon finely chopped
flat-leaf parsley leaves
1 tablespoon finely chopped
chives

SERVES 4

To make the anchovy butter, place all the ingredients in a bowl and mix well with a fork until smooth. Transfer to the centre of a large square of baking paper, roll up into a cylinder and place in the fridge to chill until ready to serve.

While the butter chills, preheat the barbecue grill to hot.

Drizzle the asparagus with the oil, season well with salt and pepper and toss to coat.

Cook the asparagus for 3–4 minutes, turning with your tongs to cook evenly, until slightly softened and charred on the outside.

To serve, arrange the asparagus on a platter, sprinkle with the chilli flakes and season well with salt and pepper. Slice the chilled anchovy butter into rounds and use it to top the asparagus. Dig in.

For a long time, cauliflower was my favourite vegetable, but I have to say pumpkin has now secured that top spot in my heart (and on my tastebuds) due to its natural sweetness and versatility. This recipe is a really lovely way to celebrate this vegetable – a classic pairing of pumpkin and pine nuts with the addition of a simple pesto.

PUMPKIN WEDGES *with* PINE NUT PESTO

600 g kent pumpkin, deseeded
  and cut into wedges
2 tablespoons extra-virgin
  olive oil
2 teaspoons smoked or
  sweet paprika
2 garlic cloves, crushed

PINE NUT PESTO

90 g (½ cup) pine nuts, lightly
  toasted
2 cups basil leaves
2 small garlic cloves, peeled
  and halved
125 ml (½ cup) extra-virgin
  olive oil

SERVES 4

For the pesto, place the pine nuts, basil and garlic in the bowl of a food processor and process until finely chopped. With the motor running, gradually add the oil in a thin, steady stream until well combined. Transfer to a bowl and place in the fridge until ready to serve.

Preheat the barbecue grill to medium–hot.

Place the pumpkin, olive oil, paprika and garlic in a large bowl and toss well to coat.

Place the pumpkin on the grill and cook for 6–8 minutes on each side or until soft, tender and charred on the outside.

Transfer the pumpkin to a platter, top with generous dollops of the pine nut pesto and serve.

Mushrooms are a favourite of mine – they're full of flavour, but they also pack a serious nutritional punch when it comes to good bacteria to promote gut health. Any recipe that is good for you while also being seriously delicious is a win-win.

MOREISH MUSHIES *with* SMASHED PUMPKIN

3 tablespoons extra-virgin
   olive oil
3 garlic cloves, crushed
2 teaspoons finely chopped
   rosemary leaves
1 teaspoon finely chopped thyme
   leaves, plus extra sprigs
   to serve
sea salt and freshly ground
   black pepper
4 large portobello mushrooms
   (about 150 g each), stems
   trimmed, cleaned
lemon wedges, to serve

SMASHED PUMPKIN

700 g butternut pumpkin,
   peeled and roughly chopped
sea salt
3 tablespoons extra-virgin
   olive oil
2 tablespoons coconut cream
2 tablespoons hulled tahini
2 garlic cloves, crushed
1 teaspoon ground cumin
½ teaspoon chilli powder
finely grated zest and juice
   of 1 lemon
freshly ground black pepper

SERVES 4

Start with the smashed pumpkin. Place the pumpkin, 1 teaspoon of salt and about 3 tablespoons of water in a saucepan over medium heat. Cover and cook, stirring occasionally, for 10–15 minutes, until very soft. (Add a little more water if the pumpkin becomes dry.)

Transfer the pumpkin to a large bowl and allow to cool. Roughly mash, then stir through the remaining ingredients. Season with salt and pepper to taste and set aside.

Preheat the barbecue grill to medium–hot.

Place the olive oil, garlic, rosemary and thyme in a large bowl and whisk well to combine. Season with salt and pepper and spoon over the mushrooms, using your hands to gently coat them all over with the oil. Set aside to marinate for 10 minutes.

Shake off any excess oil from the mushrooms, place on the grill and cook for 8–10 minutes, turning halfway through, or until beautifully charred on the outside. Transfer to a wooden board and cut each into thirds.

To serve, spread the smashed pumpkin onto plates, then top with the mushrooms and a few extra sprigs of thyme. Season well with salt and pepper and serve with lemon wedges for squeezing over.

I love cooking zucchini on the barbecue because it doesn't require any pre-cooking and it chars really quickly. Plus, it pairs so well with bold flavours, such as lemon and chilli. You'll notice I use two different varieties of zucchini here for different shapes and textures, but simply use whatever type you can get your hands on. I've gotta say, yellow zucchini look incredible with this dish, too!

CHARRED ZUCCHINI *with* LEMON *and* CHILLI

3 green zucchini (about 500 g in total), finely sliced lengthways

3 grey zucchini (about 500 g in total), finely sliced lengthways

finely grated zest and juice of 1 lemon

1 garlic clove, crushed

3 tablespoons extra-virgin olive oil

sea salt and freshly ground black pepper

½ cup flat-leaf parsley leaves, finely chopped

2 tablespoons roughly chopped pecans

1 teaspoon dried chilli flakes

SERVES 4

Preheat the barbecue grill to hot.

Cook the zucchini, in batches, for 2–3 minutes on each side or until charred and cooked through (you don't want to overdo them as they will become too soft to work with).

Meanwhile, place the lemon zest and juice, garlic and oil in a large bowl, season generously with salt and pepper and mix well.

Add the charred zucchini to the bowl and gently toss. Transfer to a platter, scatter over the parsley, pecans and chilli flakes and serve.

Covered in spicy goodness, this cajun grilled corn recipe is a real crowd pleaser.
I think they're great straight up like this, but don't forget corn is also awesome sliced
off the cob and used in salads and salsas, or as a simple side.

CAJUN CORN *on the* COB

4 sweetcorn cobs
125 ml (½ cup) extra-virgin
    olive oil
1 red onion, finely diced
2 garlic cloves, crushed

CAJUN SEASONING

3 teaspoons hot paprika
2 teaspoons dried chilli flakes
2 teaspoons garlic powder
2 teaspoons sea salt
1 teaspoon onion powder
1 teaspoon cayenne pepper
1 teaspoon dried thyme
1 teaspoon dried oregano
1 teaspoon freshly ground
    black pepper

SERVES 4

Prepare the corn by giving it a good clean and removing the husks.
Place the corn in a large bowl, cover with water and soak for a few hours
to soften it before grilling.

For the cajun seasoning, mix all the ingredients in a small bowl.

Combine 3 tablespoons of the cajun seasoning with the olive oil, onion
and garlic. Mix well to combine and set aside.

Preheat the barbecue grill to medium.

Place the corn on the grill and cook for 10–12 minutes, turning regularly.
During the last 5 minutes of cooking, baste with the cajun seasoning and
olive oil mixture. Once lovely and charred, remove from the grill and serve.

Any leftover cajun seasoning can be
stored in an airtight jar in the pantry
for up to 3 months and is delicious
sprinkled on pretty much any veg
that you are planning to throw on
the barbecue!

Originating in the Middle East, baba ganoush is similar to hummus but calls for grilled or roasted eggplant instead of chickpeas. I love fleshing out my recipes with nutrient-dense ingredients, so I've turned this ganoush into a green version by adding rich, creamy avocado.

EPIC EGGPLANT *with* GREEN GANOUSH

6 small eggplants, quartered
   lengthways
1 garlic bulb, halved horizontally
2 tablespoons extra-virgin
   olive oil
1 handful of mint leaves, to serve
sea salt and freshly ground
   black pepper

GREEN GANOUSH

2 small eggplants
3 tablespoons unsweetened
   coconut yoghurt or coconut
   cream
1 avocado
2 tablespoons hulled tahini
finely grated zest and juice
   of 1 lemon
sea salt and freshly ground
   black pepper

PISTACHIO DUKKAH

3 tablespoons sesame seeds
70 g (½ cup) pistachio kernels,
   finely chopped
2 teaspoons ground coriander
2 teaspoons ground cumin
½ teaspoon freshly ground
   black pepper
1 teaspoon sea salt

SERVES 4

Preheat the barbecue grill to hot.

Place the quartered eggplant, garlic bulb and whole eggplants for the green ganoush on the grill. Cook for 4–5 minutes on each side or until really charred and softened, basting the quartered eggplant with the olive oil as you go. Remove and allow to cool. Once cool enough to handle, pop the charred garlic cloves out of the skin.

For the green ganoush, peel the whole eggplants and discard the skin. Place the eggplant flesh in a food processor, then add half the grilled garlic, the coconut yoghurt or coconut cream, avocado, tahini and lemon zest and juice. Season with salt and pepper and process until smooth. Place in the fridge until ready to use (it will keep for up to 5 days).

For the dukkah, place the sesame seeds in a non-stick frying pan over medium heat. Cook, stirring, for 5 minutes or until toasted and golden. Add the pistachio, ground spices and pepper and cook, stirring, for 1 minute, or until aromatic. Stir in the salt and set aside to cool.

Divide the green ganoush among plates and top with the eggplant wedges. Sprinkle with the dukkah and mint leaves, season with salt and pepper and enjoy.

It's no secret that I am a lover of all things cauliflower, and I view each cookbook as another opportunity to introduce you guys to new, delicious ways of enjoying it. This time, I was playing around with flavours and was blown away by how well a smoky romesco sauce paired with cauliflower, so I just had to share it. The total cooking time for the cauli will vary based on how thick you slice the steaks and the heat of your grill, so please check as you go and simply add or subtract a few minutes either way to ensure it is cooked to perfection.

CHARRED CAULIFLOWER *with* REALLY GOOD ROMESCO

2 heads of cauliflower

2 tablespoons extra-virgin olive oil

finely grated zest and juice of 2 lemons

2 garlic cloves, crushed

1 teaspoon honey, maple syrup or monk fruit syrup

sea salt

½ teaspoon dried chilli flakes

3 tablespoons finely chopped flat-leaf parsley leaves

3 tablespoons walnuts or pecans, toasted and roughly chopped

1 lemon, cut into wedges

REALLY GOOD ROMESCO

2 large red capsicums, quartered, deseeded and membranes removed

80 g (½ cup) blanched almonds

1 garlic clove, quartered

2 tablespoons red wine vinegar

1 tablespoon extra-virgin olive oil

1 tablespoon tomato paste

2 teaspoons dried chilli flakes

sea salt and freshly ground black pepper

SERVES 4

Preheat the barbecue grill to hot.

For the romesco sauce, place the capsicum on the grill and cook for 4–5 minutes on each side or until the skin is blistered and blackened. Transfer to a bowl, cover and set aside for 5 minutes.

Remove and discard the skin, then place the capsicum in a food processor with the almonds and garlic and process until finely chopped. Add the vinegar, olive oil, tomato paste and chilli flakes. Season well with salt and pepper. Process until the mixture is combined, then set aside.

Cut off the stem at the bottom of each head of cauliflower so that they sit flat on a chopping board. Cut each one in half, then trim off the rounded edges to create four thick steaks. Alternatively, you can cut each head of cauliflower into four thinner steaks, which will cook slightly faster if you are short on time. (Make sure you save any offcuts from creating your steaks for another use, such as drizzling with olive oil and roasting in the oven until lovely and crispy!)

In a large, shallow bowl, mix the olive oil, lemon zest and juice, garlic and sweetener of choice. Season well with salt, then add the cauliflower and gently toss with your hands to coat.

Reduce the barbecue grill to medium.

Place the cauliflower on the grill, close the lid and cook for 5–6 minutes or until beginning to char. Brush any remaining marinade over the cauli, then turn, close the lid and cook for a further 5–6 minutes or until charred on the outside, golden brown around the edges and tender inside. You can tell when your cauliflower steaks are done by gently inserting a fork – if it glides in easily without much resistance, you're good to go. Remove from the grill.

To serve, spread the romesco sauce on a large platter, then top with the cauliflower steaks. Sprinkle with the chilli flakes, parsley and walnuts or pecans. Serve hot with the lemon wedges for squeezing over.

I really believe vegetables come alive when roasted on the barbecue. It gives them a texture and flavour that really can't be replicated any other way – just think of the difference between steamed broccoli and broccoli cooked over hot flames. I also love the versatility of this macadamia crumb. This recipe makes enough for you to have leftovers to keep in the fridge and sprinkle on top of all kinds of dishes.

BARBECUED BROCCOLI
with MACADAMIA CRUMB

3 tablespoons extra-virgin olive oil

¼ teaspoon dried chilli flakes, plus extra to serve

sea salt and freshly ground black pepper

2 heads of broccoli (about 800 g in total), cut into large florets

angel hair chilli threads, to serve (optional)

1 lemon, cut into wedges

MACADAMIA CRUMB

1 tablespoon extra-virgin olive oil

2 garlic cloves, crushed

2 teaspoons ground coriander

2 teaspoons ground cumin

1 teaspoon curry powder

finely grated zest of 1 lemon

1 teaspoon dried rosemary leaves

160 g (1 cup) macadamias, roughly chopped

½ teaspoon smoked paprika

1 teaspoon sea salt

½ teaspoon dried chilli flakes

1 tablespoon maple syrup

SERVES 4

For the macadamia crumb, heat the olive oil in a frying pan over medium–low heat. Add the garlic, coriander, cumin, curry powder, lemon zest and rosemary and cook, stirring, for 1–2 minutes or until fragrant. Add the macadamias and continue cooking, stirring to coat everything evenly, for a few minutes to lightly toast the nuts. Add the paprika, salt, chilli flakes and maple syrup (the maple syrup will bubble away nicely). Stir to coat everything and keep cooking for a further minute or so. Remove from the heat and transfer to a dish or bowl to cool completely and go crunchy.

Preheat the barbecue grill to medium.

In a large bowl, whisk the olive oil, chilli flakes and a generous amount of salt and pepper. Add the broccoli and toss well to coat. Set aside to marinate for 5–10 minutes.

Place the broccoli on the grill and sprinkle lightly with a little more salt. Grill for 10–12 minutes, flipping every 2 minutes and basting with any remaining oil, until tender and charred.

Top with ⅓ cup of the macadamia crumb, some extra dried chilli flakes and angel hair chilli, if desired. Serve with the lemon wedges.

Leftover macadamia crumb can be stored in an airtight container in the fridge for up to 4 weeks. Sprinkle it on roasted veggies, salads or grilled fish.

Angel hair chilli threads are very fine strands of dried red chilli. They are available from specialty food stores and online.

When experimenting with this recipe, I found the best way to grill cabbage is to cut it into big fat wedges, leaving the core intact. This helps to keep all the leaves together as it grills and also gives you plenty of surface area for charring, which is where so much of the flavour comes from.

CHARRED CABBAGE *with* ZESTY HERB OIL

1 green cabbage, cut into
   6 wedges, with core left intact
2 tablespoons extra-virgin
   olive oil, plus extra for drizzling
sea salt and freshly ground
   black pepper

ZESTY HERB OIL

3 tablespoons extra-virgin
   olive oil
finely grated zest and juice
   of 4 limes
3 tablespoons sugar-free
   fish sauce
3 tablespoons maple syrup or
   coconut nectar
3 garlic cloves, crushed
2 teaspoons dried chilli flakes
2 tablespoons finely chopped
   mint leaves
2 tablespoons finely chopped
   coriander leaves

SERVES 4

Prepare the barbecue for indirect cooking (see page 17), preheating the grill to very hot and leaving the other side off.

For the zesty herb oil, place the olive oil, lime zest and juice, fish sauce, maple syrup or coconut nectar, garlic and chilli flakes in a bowl and whisk well. Stir in the herbs and set aside.

Rub the cabbage wedges with the olive oil, then place them on the hot side of the grill. Close the lid and cook for 2–3 minutes on each side or until they soften and caramelise around the edges and develop some lovely char marks. Once you are happy with the level of char, use your tongs to turn once more so that the outside of each wedge is on the grill. Close the lid and cook for 1–2 minutes. Carefully move the cabbage to the cooler side of the grill, making sure you don't break the wedges as they will have softened. Close the lid and cook for a final 4–5 minutes or until the wedges are completely charred and warmed all the way through.

Transfer the cabbage to a large bowl, drizzle with a little olive oil and season well with salt and pepper. Serve on a large platter with the zesty herb oil spooned over the top.

Nothing beats whole-roasted cauli and broccoli. When cooked like this, they get a lovely charred exterior and a soft, warm centre that make the perfect plant-based main meal or side to any barbecued dish.

BARBECUED WHOLE CAULI *and* BROCCOLI

1 head of cauliflower

1 head of broccoli

100 g unsalted butter, softened

4 garlic cloves, crushed

5 sprigs of thyme, leaves picked

3 sprigs of rosemary, leaves picked and finely chopped

1 teaspoon sea salt, plus extra to serve

½ teaspoon freshly ground black pepper, plus extra to serve

3 tablespoons extra-virgin olive oil

3 tablespoons Pistachio Dukkah (see page 44)

SERVES 4

Prepare the barbecue for indirect cooking (see page 17), preheating the grill to medium and leaving the other side completely off.

Cut the bases of both the cauliflower and broccoli to create a flat surface that will sit easily on the barbecue.

Place the butter, garlic, thyme, rosemary, salt and pepper in a bowl and mix well. Use your hands to coat the cauliflower and broccoli with the butter mixture, making sure they are both covered well.

Place the cauliflower on the grill, close the lid and cook for 1–1½ hours, until golden brown and really soft. Place the broccoli on the grill after about 30 minutes, close the lid and cook for 40–50 minutes, or until lovely and tender. If either the cauliflower or broccoli start to get too dark on the outside during cooking, cover them with some foil.

Transfer the cauliflower and broccoli to a platter, drizzle over the olive oil and season well with salt and pepper. Top with the pistachio dukkah and serve immediately.

When I first started getting into healthy cooking as a young personal trainer more than 15 years ago, sweet potatoes were my go-to for both flavour and nutrition. They're really versatile and good for your health, plus they taste absolutely great on the barbecue.

ROASTED BABY SWEET POTATO SMASH

8 baby sweet potatoes

3 tablespoons extra-virgin olive oil

4 garlic cloves, crushed

sea salt and freshly ground black pepper

3 tablespoons finely chopped flat-leaf parsley leaves

1 tablespoon dried chilli flakes

SERVES 4

Preheat the barbecue grill to medium–low.

Tightly wrap the sweet potatoes individually in foil and place them on the grill, then close the lid and cook for 30–40 minutes. Check to see if they are done by squeezing with your tongs – if they give a little they're good to go. Depending on the size of your sweet potatoes, they may need another 5–10 minutes.

Once they're done, open the foil at the top and use a fork to smash the potatoes open, revealing the flesh inside. Drizzle with the olive oil, top with the garlic and season with salt and pepper (leave the foil open so the tops of the potatoes can get nice and brown at the next stage).

Increase the barbecue grill to hot.

Close the lid and cook for a further 5–10 minutes, until the tops are golden brown and the garlic has softened.

Remove the sweet potatoes from the foil, transfer to a platter and sprinkle over the parsley and chilli flakes to finish.

If there is one dish that pleases everyone in the family it would have to be crispy, golden-brown roast potatoes. Try whipping these ones out at your next barbecue and see how your loved ones react when they taste the salty, rosemary goodness here!

PERFECT ROAST POTATOES
with ROSEMARY

4 large red potatoes, peeled and quartered

3 tablespoons extra-virgin olive oil

2 tablespoons finely chopped rosemary leaves

finely grated zest and juice of 1 lemon

2 teaspoons sea salt

1 teaspoon freshly ground black pepper

SERVES 4

Prepare the barbecue for indirect cooking (see page 17), preheating the grill to medium and leaving the other side completely off.

Bring a saucepan of salted water to the boil over high heat (use your side burner if your barbecue has one). Add the potato, reduce the heat to medium and simmer for 20 minutes or until just cooked enough to be pierced with a fork.

Drain thoroughly (you don't want the potato carrying excess liquid when it hits the barbecue or it won't crisp up) and transfer to a large bowl. Add the olive oil, rosemary, lemon zest and juice, salt and pepper, and mix well so that the potato is evenly coated.

Place the potato on the side of the grill that is turned off, close the lid and roast for 30–40 minutes or until golden brown and a little crispy around the edges.

Transfer the potato to the hot grill and cook over direct heat for about 4–5 minutes or until lovely and charred.

Transfer to a platter, season generously with salt and pepper and serve.

These potatoes go really well with my whole baked snapper (see page 77) or chermoula lamb shoulder with tahini sauce (see page 154).

VERY GOOD VEG

Most barbecues I host have a few guests asking for more plant-based alternatives to the standard steak and snags. This recipe is perfect either as an entree or a main meal for guests looking for more vegetables on their plate. Got a vegan friend over? Swap the eggs out for flax eggs (see below) and you're good to go!

FANTASTIC FRITTERS
with SMASHED AVO

1 large zucchini
250 g (2 cups) coarsely grated
    sweet potato
¼ red onion, grated
55 g (½ cup) almond meal,
    plus extra if needed
1 tablespoon dried chilli flakes
pinch of sea salt
2 eggs
3 tablespoons coconut oil, butter
    or ghee

SMASHED AVO

2 avocados
finely grated zest and juice
    of 1 lemon
pinch of sea salt

TO SERVE

Aioli (see page 83)
lemon wedges
coriander sprigs
sea salt
dried chilli flakes

SERVES 4

Grate the zucchini and place it on a clean tea towel or muslin cloth. Wrap it up, hold it over the sink and squeeze out the excess liquid until the zucchini is dry. Alternatively, place the grated zucchini in a colander and squeeze it out over the sink.

Place the zucchini, sweet potato, onion, almond meal, chilli flakes, salt and eggs in a large bowl and mix well to form a batter. If it is looking a little wet, add some more almond meal to help it come together.

Preheat the barbecue flat plate to medium.

Melt 1 tablespoon of your preferred cooking fat on the flat plate. Working in batches of five or six at a time, spoon heaped tablespoons of the batter onto the flat plate in loose rounds and press down lightly to form fritters. Cook for 2–3 minutes on each side until crisp, then transfer to some paper towel to remove any excess oil. Repeat with the remaining fat and batter.

For the smashed avo, place the avocados, lemon zest and juice and salt in a bowl, then use a fork to mash until combined. You can leave it nice and chunky or keep pressing with the fork for a smoother consistency.

Divide the fritters and smashed avo among plates and serve with dollops of aioli, lemon wedges and a scattering of coriander sprigs. Season with salt and sprinkle over some extra dried chilli flakes to finish. Enjoy!

To make a flax egg, mix 1½ tablespoons of flaxseed meal with 3 tablespoons of water in a bowl. Transfer to the fridge and leave for 15–30 minutes, or until the mixture has begun to thicken and is all goopy, like an egg. For more flax eggs, just scale up the quantities (for two flax eggs, double them, and so on). And if you don't like flax? Simply substitute the ground flax for the same quantity of ground chia seeds. Too easy!

Sensational SEAFOOD

Ocean trout fillets look almost identical to salmon fillets, both being pink, firm-fleshed fish. Ocean trout has a very mild flavour and, compared to salmon, is a heartier, meatier, sweeter tasting fish with a higher amount of healthy oil. To be fair, they're quite interchangeable in this particular recipe, so give it a go with whatever you can get your hands on.

MEXICAN-SPICED OCEAN TROUT with AVOCADO SALSA

4 x 170 g ocean trout fillets, deboned and skin on
2 tablespoons coconut or extra-virgin olive oil
sea salt and freshly ground black pepper
coriander sprigs, to serve
lime wedges, to serve

MEXICAN SPICE RUB

¼ teaspoon sea salt
¼ teaspoon ground cumin
¼ teaspoon chilli powder
¼ teaspoon smoked paprika

AVOCADO SALSA

2 avocados, diced
½ red onion, finely chopped
3 tablespoons extra-virgin olive or avocado oil
finely grated zest and juice of 1 lime
1 tablespoon finely chopped coriander leaves
1 long red chilli, finely chopped

SERVES 4

For the avocado salsa, place all the ingredients in a bowl and mix gently, keeping the avocado chunky.

In a small bowl, mix the Mexican spice rub ingredients.

Using a sharp knife, score the ocean trout fillets along the skin and season well with the spice rub, rubbing it into the skin and the score marks.

Preheat the barbecue grill to medium–hot and grease with the oil.

Cook the ocean trout, skin-side down and with the lid closed, for 3–4 minutes or until the skin is golden brown and crispy and the fish is beginning to cook through. Turn and continue to cook for another 2–3 minutes or until cooked to your liking. Remove from the heat and allow to rest for 2 minutes.

Place the ocean trout on plates and season well with salt and pepper. Spoon over the avocado salsa and serve with some coriander sprigs and lime wedges.

Nothing is quite as simple or delicious as grilled white fish with a buttery herb sauce. This recipe takes the cake when it comes to putting beautiful flavours together on a plate with ease.

GRILLED BARRAMUNDI
with HERB BUTTER

2 baby cos lettuce, cut into rough chunks

1 bunch of radishes, trimmed and finely sliced

pinch of sea salt

2 tablespoons extra-virgin olive oil

4 x 170 g barramundi fillets, deboned and skin on

freshly ground black pepper

lemon wedges, to serve

HERB BUTTER

125 g unsalted butter

1 bunch of chives, roughly chopped

1 bunch of dill, fronds picked and roughly chopped

1 bunch of flat-leaf parsley, leaves picked and roughly chopped

100 g capers, rinsed and drained

finely grated zest and juice of 1 lemon

sea salt and freshly ground black pepper

SERVES 4

For the herb butter, melt the butter in a saucepan over low heat (use your side burner if your barbecue has one). Add the chives, dill, parsley and capers and stir to combine, then remove from the heat and stir in the lemon zest and juice. Season with salt and pepper to taste, then set aside until needed (if your butter sets a little, simply heat on low until runny again for serving).

Preheat the barbecue flat plate to medium.

Place the cos lettuce, radish, salt and 1 tablespoon of the olive oil in a bowl and toss. Set aside.

Lightly coat the barramundi fillets with the remaining olive oil and season with salt and pepper. Place the fillets on the flat plate, skin-side down, close the lid and cook for 7 minutes or until the skin is golden and crispy. Using tongs, carefully flip the barramundi over and cook for a further 4–5 minutes or until cooked through (you'll know it's good when the flesh starts to flake apart).

Place the barramundi on serving plates, arrange the cos salad next to it, spoon the herb butter over the lot and serve with some lemon wedges.

When I was a kid I was *addicted* to all things teriyaki! At the time, Japanese restaurants were popping up everywhere and my go-to was teriyaki salmon, so here's my take on it with a few healthy tweaks to the traditional teriyaki sauce. This is delicious on its own, but also goes really well with a simple cauliflower rice (see below) or my magnificent mango salad (see page 208).

TERIYAKI SALMON SKEWERS

1 x 600 g salmon fillet, deboned, skin off and cut into 3 cm pieces

600 g pineapple, cut into 3 cm pieces

2 onions, cut into 2.5 cm wedges

8 bamboo skewers, soaked in cold water for at least 20 minutes before using

extra-virgin olive oil, for greasing

TERIYAKI MARINADE

125 ml (½ cup) coconut aminos

125 ml (½ cup) tamari

3 tablespoons coconut sugar

2 tablespoons finely grated ginger

1 red onion, grated

1 tablespoon crushed garlic

½ teaspoon dried chilli flakes

2 tablespoons extra-virgin olive oil

SERVES 4

For the teriyaki marinade, place the coconut aminos, tamari and coconut sugar in a large bowl and mix until the sugar is completely dissolved. Add the remaining ingredients and mix well.

Place the cubes of salmon in the bowl of marinade and gently mix to coat completely. Cover and place in the fridge to marinate for 1–2 hours.

When ready to cook, remove the salmon from the bowl and transfer the remaining marinade to a small saucepan over high heat. Bring to the boil, then reduce the heat and simmer for 8–10 minutes or until slightly thickened. Remove from the heat and set aside.

Preheat the barbecue grill to hot.

Thread the salmon, pineapple and onion pieces onto the prepared skewers. Lightly oil the grill, then add the skewers and cook for 3–4 minutes. Baste with the reserved marinade, flip over and cook for a further 3–4 minutes, basting frequently, until the salmon is just cooked through (it will keep cooking when removed from the heat). Serve immediately.

To make cauliflower rice, place the roughly chopped stalks and florets of 1 head of cauliflower in a food processor and pulse into rice-like pieces (this usually takes six to eight pulses). Melt 2 tablespoons of coconut oil in a large frying pan over medium heat, add the cauliflower and sauté for 4–6 minutes or until softened. Season with salt to taste.

I feel like food on sticks is just so much more fun to eat. Here there's a bonus too, as the sticks allow you to really dunk deeply into the beautiful coconut yoghurt dipping sauce.

BANGIN' BARBECUED PRAWNS on a STICK

24 large raw prawns, peeled and deveined, with tails left intact
8 metal skewers
sea salt
125 g (½ cup) unsweetened coconut yoghurt
1 handful of coriander leaves, chopped (optional)

SMOKY TAMARI MARINADE

3 tablespoons tomato paste
1 tablespoon tamari or coconut aminos
1 garlic clove, crushed
1 teaspoon smoked paprika
1 teaspoon ground cumin
finely grated zest and juice of 1 lemon
2 tablespoons honey, maple syrup or monk fruit syrup
1 tablespoon extra-virgin olive oil

SERVES 4

Mix all the marinade ingredients in a large bowl. Add the prawns and combine well. Cover and marinate in the fridge for at least 30 minutes or overnight if you have the time.

When ready to cook, preheat the barbecue grill to medium–hot.

Lift the prawns out of the marinade (reserving any leftover marinade) and thread three prawns onto each skewer. Season with salt and grill for 2–3 minutes, turning once, until just cooked through.

Meanwhile, heat the remaining marinade in a small saucepan over medium heat (use your side burner if your barbecue has one). Remove from the heat and leave it to cool slightly before mixing with the yoghurt and coriander (if using).

Serve the prawn skewers with the yoghurt sauce for dipping.

Salmon is one of the most popular types of fish in Australia, and for good reason – it's good for you and tastes great. That said, for the best fillets in the bunch, check where they've been sourced from. The flesh should be lovely and pink, and if it smells at all like seafood, move on.

CRISPY SKIN SALMON *with* BUTTERY PEA SMASH

2 tablespoons extra-virgin olive oil, plus extra for drizzling
4 x 170 g salmon fillets, deboned and skin on
sea salt and freshly ground black pepper
1 lemon, cut into wedges

HERB SALAD

2 shallots, finely sliced
1 teaspoon coconut sugar
finely grated zest and juice of 1 lemon
sea salt and freshly ground black pepper
1 cup loosely packed mint leaves
1 cup loosely packed flat-leaf parsley leaves

BUTTERY PEA SMASH

40 g unsalted butter
1 garlic clove, finely grated
500 g frozen baby peas
80 ml (⅓ cup) chicken broth or water
3 tablespoons coconut cream

SERVES 4

For the herb salad, place the shallot, coconut sugar and lemon zest and juice in a small bowl and mix well. Season to taste and leave to soften for 10–15 minutes.

Meanwhile, for the buttery pea smash, warm the butter in a saucepan over medium heat (use your side burner if your barbecue has one), add the garlic and fry gently until softened, about 1–2 minutes. Add the peas and broth or water, bring to the boil and cook until the peas are just tender, about 2–3 minutes. Remove from the heat, add the coconut cream and puree with a hand-held blender until lovely and smooth. Cover with foil to keep warm and set aside.

Preheat the barbecue flat plate to medium–hot and grease with the olive oil.

Place the salmon on the flat plate, skin-side down, and cook for 3–4 minutes or until the skin is crispy and the flesh has begun to cook through. Using tongs, carefully turn the salmon over and continue to cook for about 1 minute for medium salmon or longer until it is cooked to your liking. Transfer to a plate and rest for a few minutes.

Add the herbs to the softened shallot mixture, toss well and season to taste again.

To serve, spoon the buttery pea smash onto plates. Arrange the salmon on top and the herb salad on the side. Drizzle with a little more olive oil, season with salt and pepper and serve with the lemon wedges on the side.

Sardines are an incredibly delicious, healthy and sustainable choice of seafood. A little platter of these makes the most delicious entree or serve them with one of my salads, such as the charred cos with green tahini dressing (see page 186), to turn it into a hearty and filling main.

SIMPLE SARDINES *with* GARLIC *and* ROSEMARY

2 tablespoons extra-virgin olive oil, plus extra to serve

3 garlic cloves, finely sliced

1 tablespoon smoked paprika, plus extra to serve

1 lemon, zested and cut into wedges to serve

4 rosemary sprigs, leaves picked and bruised

1 long red chilli, deseeded and finely chopped

sea salt and freshly ground black pepper

8 large or 16 small sardines, gutted and cleaned

SERVES 4

Place the olive oil, garlic, paprika, lemon zest, rosemary and chilli in a small bowl. Season with a little salt and pepper and mix well, then pour into a baking dish.

Add the sardines to the baking dish and toss well to coat. Cover and place in the fridge to marinate for 2–3 hours.

Preheat the barbecue grill to medium–hot.

Place the sardines on the grill, close the lid and cook for 8–10 minutes, turning halfway through, or until caramelised and charred.

Transfer the sardines to a platter, drizzle over a little more olive oil and sprinkle with some more paprika. Squeeze over the lemon wedges and serve immediately.

Baking fish whole is a great technique as the fish takes on all the nutrients and flavour from the bones during the cooking process. I love using whole baby snapper in this recipe, so that each person has their own delicious fish to devour.

WHOLE BAKED SNAPPER
with CHARRED HERB OIL

4 x whole baby snapper (300–400 g each), gutted and cleaned
1 lemon, finely sliced into discs
8 flat-leaf parsley sprigs
100 g unsalted butter, cubed
sea salt and freshly ground black pepper
Charred Lemon Halves (see page 114), to serve

CHARRED HERB OIL

250 ml (1 cup) extra-virgin olive oil
2 bunches of flat-leaf parsley
1 bunch of mint
1 bunch of coriander
8 spring onions
finely grated zest and juice of 2 lemons
1 tablespoon dijon mustard
1 teaspoon dried chilli flakes
¼ red onion, finely diced
sea salt and freshly ground black pepper

SERVES 4

Preheat the barbecue grill to hot.

For the charred herb oil, lightly drizzle 1 tablespoon of the olive oil over the bunches of herbs and spring onions. Place on the grill and cook for 2–3 minutes on each side or until they start to char nicely around the edges. Transfer to a wooden board and leave to cool slightly. Once cool enough to handle, roughly chop and transfer to a bowl. Stir through all the remaining ingredients and set aside until ready to serve.

Reduce the barbecue to medium–hot and close the lid.

Rinse the fish inside and out under cold running water and pat dry with paper towel. Make three shallow cuts, 1 cm deep, in the thickest part of each fish side.

Place a 30 cm x 40 cm piece of baking paper in the centre of a similar-sized piece of foil. Repeat to make four of these.

Divide the lemon slices and parsley sprigs among the fish cavities. Divide half the butter among the fish cavities and use the remainder to top the fish, then season well with salt and pepper.

Working with one fish at a time, place it on the prepared paper, bring two sides of the foil up towards the centre and then fold the foil edges to create a seal. Roll up the remaining ends of the foil to enclose the fish securely.

Place the fish on the barbecue, close the lid and cook for 8–10 minutes or until cooked through.

Divide the fish parcels among plates, unwrap and serve with the herb oil and charred lemon.

I have a love–hate relationship with swordfish because, while I adore its flavour and meaty texture, it was a swordfish dish that got me eliminated from *My Kitchen Rules* in the finals! I was one step away from the grand final ... so consider this my redemption dish!

SATAY SWORDFISH SKEWERS

160 ml (⅔ cup) tamari or
   coconut aminos
2 tablespoons coconut sugar
600 g swordfish fillets, cut into
   3 cm pieces
8 bamboo skewers, soaked
   in cold water for at least
   20 minutes before using
1 lime, cut into wedges

SATAY DRESSING

80 ml (⅓ cup) extra-virgin olive
   or macadamia oil
4 garlic cloves, finely chopped
2 long red chillies, deseeded and
   finely chopped
2 cm piece of ginger, grated
1 red onion, finely chopped
3 tablespoons coconut sugar
75 g (½ cup) unsalted peanuts,
   toasted and roughly chopped
juice of 2 limes and finely grated
   zest of 1
2 tablespoons sugar-free
   fish sauce
½ cup coriander leaves, roughly
   chopped

SERVES 4

Get started by marinating the swordfish. Place the tamari or coconut aminos and coconut sugar in a large bowl and whisk until the sugar is completely dissolved (it will look like a sticky caramel). Add the swordfish and gently toss to coat evenly. Set aside at room temperature to marinate for 15 minutes.

For the satay dressing, heat 1 tablespoon of the oil in a small frying pan over medium heat. Add the garlic, chilli, ginger and red onion and cook, stirring, for 5–6 minutes or until golden brown and softened. Add the coconut sugar and cook, stirring occasionally, for 3–4 minutes or until aromatic. Remove from the heat, then add the remaining oil, peanuts, lime zest and juice, fish sauce, coriander and 1 tablespoon of water. Mix well, then transfer to a serving bowl and set aside.

Preheat the barbecue grill to hot.

Thread the swordfish onto the prepared skewers and grill for about 2 minutes on each side or until charred and just cooked through. (Don't forget it will keep cooking when removed from the heat.)

Transfer the skewers to a platter and serve with the satay dressing and lime wedges for squeezing over.

When I first started to take cooking seriously I gave myself the challenge of trialling recipes that were outside of my comfort zone. Well, after all my practice I can now tell you confidently that preparing squid and cooking it to perfection is easier and more delicious than I ever imagined.

CHARRED GARLIC and CHILLI SQUID

800 g squid tubes, cleaned
125 ml (½ cup) extra-virgin olive oil
3 garlic cloves, crushed
2 long red chillies, deseeded and finely chopped
finely grated zest and juice of 1 lemon
sea salt and freshly ground black pepper
⅓ cup flat-leaf parsley leaves, finely chopped

AIOLI
4 egg yolks
2 teaspoons dijon mustard
2 tablespoons apple cider vinegar
juice of 1 lemon
3 garlic cloves, crushed
sea salt
400 ml extra-virgin olive or avocado oil, plus extra if needed
freshly ground black pepper

SERVES 4

For the aioli, place the egg yolks, mustard, vinegar, lemon juice, garlic and a big pinch of salt in a large bowl. Whiz together using a hand-held blender. With the hand-held blender still going, add the oil in a thin, even stream until all the oil has been incorporated and the aioli is thick and creamy. Season to taste with salt and pepper. Transfer to a bowl, cover and refrigerate until needed.

Working one at a time, place a squid tube on a chopping board and cut in half lengthways with a sharp knife. Open the cut tube out into a flat sheet, then lightly score in a criss-cross pattern in 2 mm intervals, being sure not to cut all the way through. Repeat with the remaining squid tubes, then transfer to a bowl with the olive oil, garlic, chilli and lemon zest. Cover and place in the fridge to marinate for 2 hours.

When ready to cook, preheat the barbecue grill to hot.

Season the squid well with salt and pepper, then grill for 2–3 minutes, turning halfway through with tongs, or until lightly charred and just cooked through.

Transfer the squid to a chopping board and cut into 2 cm slices. Squeeze over the lemon juice and scatter over the parsley, then transfer to a platter and serve with the aioli for dipping.

The leftover aioli can be stored in an airtight container or jar in the fridge for up to 1 week. Try adding some other flavours to mix things up – I love the combination of lemon juice and fresh dill or smoked paprika and finely chopped coriander leaves.

As much as I love snapper cooked whole as you can see on page 77, I equally love how delicate and tender the flesh is when served with crispy skin on this lovely, light zucchini base. Just one taste of this smoky vinaigrette and you'll be adding it to all your favourite recipes.

CRISPY SNAPPER FILLETS
with SMOKY VINAIGRETTE

4 zucchini, finely sliced
　　lengthways with a mandoline
¼ bunch of thyme, leaves picked
　　and chopped
2 garlic cloves, crushed
80 ml (⅓ cup) extra-virgin
　　olive oil, plus extra for
　　brushing
sea salt and freshly ground
　　black pepper
75 g (½ cup) green olives
4 x 160 g snapper fillets, skin on
micro herbs, to serve (optional)

SMOKY VINAIGRETTE

4 large truss tomatoes, halved
80 ml (⅓ cup) extra-virgin
　　olive oil
sea salt and freshly ground
　　black pepper
2 tablespoons apple cider
　　vinegar
1 garlic clove, crushed

SERVES 4

For the smoky vinaigrette, preheat the barbecue grill to hot.

Brush the tomatoes with a little olive oil and season with salt and pepper. Grill, cut-side down and turning once, for 6–8 minutes or until tender and nicely charred.

Keeping the barbecue hot, transfer the tomatoes to a sieve set over a bowl and use the back of a spoon to push through the sieve, extracting just the juice. Discard the solids and whisk the remaining ingredients into the tomato liquid until well incorporated. Season well and set aside.

Place the zucchini, thyme, garlic and olive oil in a bowl, season and toss well to combine. Cook for 5–6 minutes or until tender with good char lines, only turning once. Transfer to a plate, add the olives and loosely cover with foil to keep warm.

Preheat the barbecue flat plate to hot.

Brush the snapper fillets with a little oil, season the skin well with salt and pepper and cook, skin-side down, for 3–5 minutes or until the fish is just cooked through and the skin is crispy. Use tongs to flip and cook for a further 2–3 minutes or until cooked to your liking.

To serve, divide the charred zucchini and olives among plates and top with the snapper fillets. Drizzle over the smoky vinaigrette and scatter with micro herbs to finish, if you like.

Mango and seafood really work well together and this recipe is no exception. Feel free to swap out the salmon for ocean trout if you like, or any other firm-fleshed fish.

SUMMER SALMON SKEWERS

2 tablespoons extra-virgin
   olive oil, plus extra to serve
2 garlic cloves, crushed
1 teaspoon dried chilli flakes
1 teaspoon smoked paprika
600 g salmon fillets, deboned,
   skin off and cut into 4 cm pieces
sea salt and freshly ground
   black pepper
8 metal skewers
3 tablespoons pistachios,
   toasted and finely chopped

SUMMER SALSA

2 mangoes, diced
1 bunch of coriander, leaves
   picked and chopped
1 Lebanese cucumber, diced
10 cherry tomatoes, diced
finely grated zest and juice
   of 1 lime

SERVES 4

Whisk the olive oil, garlic, chilli flakes and paprika in a large bowl.

Pat the salmon dry with paper towel, then add it to the bowl and use your fingers to coat with the marinade. Season well with salt and pepper.

Preheat the barbecue grill to medium.

Thread the salmon onto the skewers and grill for 2–3 minutes on each side or until golden brown on the outside and just cooked through in the middle. Transfer to a plate to rest for a few minutes.

For the summer salsa, gently toss all the ingredients in a bowl.

To serve, divide the salmon skewers and summer salsa among plates, scatter over the pistachios and drizzle over a little extra olive oil to finish.

This recipe celebrates some of my favourite spices from the East – the Indian and south Asian flavours pairing so well with the spicy, zesty salsa.

INDIAN-SPICED PRAWNS

2 tablespoons red curry paste

2 tablespoons extra-virgin olive oil

finely grated zest and juice of 1 lime

2 garlic cloves, finely chopped

2 teaspoons finely grated ginger

2 teaspoons garam masala

1 teaspoon ground coriander

1 teaspoon ground turmeric

½ teaspoon dried chilli flakes

800 g raw whole unshelled banana prawns, halved lengthways with head, shell and tail intact

sea salt

MANGO SALSA

2 mangoes, diced

1 teaspoon ground cumin

1 Lebanese cucumber, diced

1 long green chilli, deseeded and finely chopped

1 red onion, finely diced

½ cup coriander leaves, roughly chopped

finely grated zest and juice of 1 lime

SERVES 4

Place the curry paste, olive oil, lime zest and juice, garlic, ginger and spices in a food processor and blitz to a smooth paste. This can also be done using a mortar and pestle if you've got one.

Transfer the marinade to a bowl, add the prawns and use your fingers to coat well. Cover and marinate in the fridge for at least 30 minutes or up to 3 hours.

While the prawns are marinating, make the mango salsa. Combine all the ingredients in a bowl, then place in the fridge until you're ready to serve.

When ready to cook, preheat the barbecue grill to medium–hot.

Grill the prawns for 3–4 minutes, turning halfway through, until charred on the outside and just cooked through (they'll continue to cook slightly once removed from the heat).

Serve immediately with the mango salsa and a good pinch of salt.

HOOKED on CHOOK

I would describe my hot sauce as spicy, fragrant and really addictive! It works great with these chicken burgers, but I strongly recommend making double because if you're anything like me, once you try it you will no doubt start putting it on absolutely *everything*!

CHARRED CHICKEN BURGERS
with LUKE'S HOT SAUCE

600 g chicken mince
1 teaspoon smoked paprika,
     plus extra to serve
1 teaspoon onion powder
½ teaspoon garlic powder
¼ teaspoon sea salt
¼ teaspoon black pepper
1 lemon, halved widthways
1 baby cos lettuce,
     leaves separated

LUKE'S HOT SAUCE

1 tablespoon coconut oil
2 tablespoons sweet paprika
1 tablespoon ground cumin
1 tablespoon ground coriander
1 red capsicum, deseeded and
     roughly chopped
½ onion, roughly chopped
2 long red chillies, deseeded
     and roughly chopped
1 bird's eye chilli
1 teaspoon finely grated ginger
finely grated zest and juice
     of 1 lemon
160 ml (⅔ cup) extra-virgin
     olive oil
sea salt and freshly ground
     black pepper

SERVES 4

To make the hot sauce, combine the coconut oil, paprika, cumin and coriander in a frying pan over medium heat and cook for 1 minute or until fragrant. Add the capsicum, onion, chillies and ginger and cook for 3–4 minutes or until the onion is soft and translucent. Stir through the lemon zest and juice, then transfer the mixture to a blender and blend until smooth. Pour in the olive oil in a slow, steady stream while blending until it is incorporated into the sauce. Season with salt and pepper to taste.

For the burgers, place the chicken mince, paprika, onion and garlic powders, salt, pepper and 3 tablespoons of Luke's hot sauce in a large bowl. Use your hands to mix everything until just combined, then shape into four even-sized patties.

Preheat the barbecue grill to medium.

Cook the burgers for 6–8 minutes on each side or until fully cooked through. Meanwhile, grill the lemon halves, cut-side down, for 1 minute on each side or until well caramelised.

To serve, place the burgers on lettuce cups, spoon over a little more hot sauce and finish with a squeeze of lemon and a sprinkle of paprika. Dig in.

Leftover hot sauce will keep in an airtight container in the fridge for up to 2 weeks and it goes beautifully with almost any grilled meat or veg.

This recipe is both a really simple South American way to cook chicken with a fresh and chunky chimichurri sauce, and an easy way to transform your next barbecue into a fiesta. I've given you instructions on how to butterfly your chook, but most butchers will do it for you ... if you ask with a smile!

BUTTERFLIED CHOOK
with CHIMICHURRI

1 x 1.8–2 kg whole chicken
2 teaspoons smoked paprika
1 teaspoon ground cumin
1 teaspoon cayenne pepper
1 teaspoon ground coriander
2 tablespoons extra-virgin
  olive oil
sea salt and freshly ground
  black pepper
1 large handful of coriander
  leaves, to serve
lime wedges, to serve

CHIMICHURRI

1 bunch of flat-leaf parsley,
  leaves picked and finely
  chopped
3 tablespoons oregano leaves,
  finely chopped
3 tablespoons extra-virgin
  olive oil
3 garlic cloves, crushed
1 teaspoon dried chilli flakes
finely grated zest and juice of
  2 lemons
2 teaspoons apple cider vinegar
sea salt and freshly ground
  black pepper

SERVES 4–6

To butterfly your chook, place it on a large chopping board, breast-side down. Using a pair of sharp kitchen scissors, cut along each side of the chicken backbone to remove it, then turn it over and press down on the middle of the chicken with the palm of your hand to open it up and flatten it out.

In a small bowl, combine the paprika, cumin, cayenne pepper, coriander and olive oil. Use your hands to massage this spice mix into the chicken, then season really generously with salt and pepper.

Preheat the barbecue grill to medium.

Place the chicken on the grill, breast-side down, close the lid and cook for 10 minutes. Turn over, close the lid and cook for a further 30 minutes, turning every 10 minutes, or until the chicken is golden brown and cooked through. Transfer to a wooden board, cover loosely with foil and leave to rest for 5–10 minutes.

While the chicken is resting, make the chimichurri. Place all the ingredients in a bowl and stir to combine. Season with salt and pepper to taste.

Chop the chicken into large pieces, then top with the chimichurri and scatter over the coriander leaves. Serve with lime wedges and my gorgeous green salad (see page 183), if you like.

This is one of my favourite flavour pairings in the book and is quite different from anything I have shared with you in the past. The sauce is really unique, with a good amount of heat and a lovely earthiness coming from the walnuts – perfect with that succulent marinated chicken!

TURKISH CHICKEN KEBABS
with WALNUT SAUCE

400 g chicken thigh fillets,
cut into 4 cm pieces
8 wooden skewers, soaked
in cold water for at least
20 minutes before using
¼ red onion, finely sliced
2 tablespoons walnuts, toasted
and roughly chopped
lemon cheeks, to serve

GARLIC AND CUMIN MARINADE

2 garlic cloves, crushed
1 teaspoon mustard powder
1 teaspoon ground cumin
1 teaspoon ground coriander
1 teaspoon dried chilli flakes
½ teaspoon ground turmeric
½ teaspoon sea salt
½ teaspoon freshly ground
black pepper
3 tablespoons extra-virgin
olive oil

WALNUT SAUCE

100 g (1 cup) walnuts
125 g (½ cup) tomato paste
3 tablespoons olive oil
4 garlic cloves, crushed
2 teaspoons sweet paprika
2 teaspoons ground cumin
2 teaspoons dried oregano
2 teaspoons dried chilli flakes
½ teaspoon freshly ground
black pepper

SERVES 4

For the garlic and cumin marinade, place all the ingredients in a large bowl and whisk until well combined.

Add the chicken to the marinade and turn to coat evenly. Thread the chicken pieces onto the prepared skewers so that they are touching but not crammed together tightly. Return the skewers to the bowl, cover and place in the fridge to marinate for at least 30 minutes or up to 3 hours for best results.

To make the walnut sauce, place all the ingredients in a food processor and blend until smooth. Transfer to a small bowl and set aside until ready to serve.

Preheat the barbecue grill to medium.

Place the kebabs on the grill, close the lid and cook for 8–10 minutes, turning once or twice, until the meat is golden brown and caramelised around the edges and cooked through.

Transfer to a platter, top with the walnut sauce, scatter over the red onion and walnuts and serve with some lemon cheeks for squeezing over.

LID ON

A chipotle is a smoke-dried ripe chilli commonly used for seasoning in Mexican and Mexican-inspired cuisines, such as Tex-Mex and Southwestern dishes. This salad encapsulates all the flavours of these regions without needing the aircraft boarding pass.

CHIPOTLE CHICKEN SALAD

3 tablespoons extra-virgin
  olive oil
2 teaspoons smoked paprika
1 teaspoon dried chilli flakes
1 teaspoon cayenne pepper
1 teaspoon ground cumin
2 garlic cloves, crushed
800 g chicken thighs, skin on
2 lemons, halved
2 baby cos lettuce, halved
  lengthways
micro herbs, to serve (optional)
sea salt and freshly ground
  black pepper

SMASHED AVO

2 avocados
finely grated zest and juice
  of 1 lemon
sea salt

SPICY TOMATO SALSA

4 tomatoes, deseeded and
  finely diced
½ red onion, finely diced
1 bunch of coriander, leaves
  picked and roughly chopped
1 long red chilli, finely chopped
finely grated zest and juice
  of 1 lime
2 tablespoons extra-virgin
  olive or avocado oil
sea salt and freshly ground
  black pepper

SERVES 4

Combine the olive oil, paprika, chilli flakes, cayenne pepper, cumin and garlic in a bowl. Add the chicken thighs and coat well. Cover, transfer to the fridge and leave to marinate for at least 10 minutes or up to 1 hour for best results.

While the chicken is marinating, prepare the smashed avo and spicy tomato salsa. For the smashed avo, place the avocado in a bowl, mash roughly with a fork and mix in the lemon zest and juice. Season well with salt and set aside. For the salsa, combine all the ingredients in a bowl.

When ready to cook, preheat the barbecue grill to hot.

Place the chicken thighs on the grill, close the lid and cook for 4 minutes. Turn the thighs carefully with tongs, add the lemon halves and cos halves, cut-side down, to the grill and cook with the lid down for another 4 minutes or until the lemons and lettuce are charred and the chicken is cooked through, with lovely, crispy skin.

Cut the cos into halves again and cut the chicken thighs into thirds, then serve both with the salsa, generous dollops of the smashed avo and the charred lemon. Scatter over some micro herbs (if using), season well with salt and pepper and enjoy.

The most cooked dish in my house is butter chicken, so I wasn't going to write a barbecue book without giving you guys a version of my all-time fave that can be done outdoors!

BUTTER CHICKEN SKEWERS

250 ml (1 cup) coconut cream

finely grated zest and juice
  of 1 lemon

1 tablespoon finely grated ginger

1 tablespoon garam masala

1 teaspoon honey, maple syrup
  or monk fruit syrup

3 garlic cloves, crushed

600 g boneless, skinless chicken
  thighs, cut into 2.5 cm cubes

1 red onion, cut into 2.5 cm chunks

2 red capsicums, cut into
  2.5 cm chunks

sea salt and freshly ground
  black pepper

8 bamboo skewers, soaked
  in cold water for at least
  20 minutes before using

2 tablespoons extra-virgin
  olive oil

3 tablespoons roughly chopped
  coriander leaves, to serve

BUTTER CHICKEN SAUCE

40 g unsalted butter

1 red onion, finely chopped

2 garlic cloves, crushed

2 teaspoons finely grated ginger

2 teaspoons garam masala

1 teaspoon ground coriander

1 teaspoon ground turmeric

500 g (2 cups) tomato passata

finely grated zest and juice
  of 1 lemon

125 ml (½ cup) coconut cream

¼ teaspoon sea salt

SERVES 4

Place the coconut cream, lemon zest and juice, ginger, garam masala, sweetener of choice and garlic in a large bowl and whisk until well combined. Add the chicken and mix well. Cover and place in the fridge to marinate for at least 30 minutes or up to 24 hours.

For the butter chicken sauce, melt the butter in a large, heavy-based frying pan over medium heat. Add the onion and cook for 4–5 minutes or until softened. Add the garlic and ginger and cook for 1–2 minutes or until softened and fragrant. Stir in the garam masala, coriander and turmeric and cook for a further 1 minute, then add the passata and lemon zest and juice, bring to a simmer and cook for 15 minutes or until slightly reduced. Stir in the coconut cream and salt and simmer for another 5 minutes or until thickened. Set aside.

Preheat the barbecue grill to medium.

Remove the chicken from the marinade and shake off any excess. In a bowl, mix the chicken, onion and capsicum and season with salt and pepper. Thread one piece of capsicum, one chunk of onion and one piece of chicken onto a prepared skewer. Repeat two more times so that you have three pieces of chicken on the skewer, then repeat with the remaining skewers.

Drizzle the skewers with the olive oil and grill for 6–8 minutes, turning regularly, until cooked through with lovely char marks on all sides.

Arrange the skewers on a platter. Warm the sauce and spoon it over the skewers, then scatter over a little chopped coriander. Season well with salt and pepper and serve with my zesty summer raita (see page 202), if you like.

These chicken fajitas are perfect for getting the whole family sharing everything at the dinner table and just digging in. I like to make up the capsicum mix and the guacamole while the chicken is marinating, as that way there's nothing much left to do once you get started on the grilling.

CHICKEN FAJITAS

600 g boneless chicken thigh
    or breast
4 garlic cloves, crushed
finely grated zest and juice
    of 2 limes
1 teaspoon hot chilli powder
1 teaspoon ground cumin
1 teaspoon ground coriander
1 teaspoon dried oregano
1 teaspoon smoked paprika
sea salt
125 ml (½ cup) extra-virgin
    olive oil, plus extra for greasing
2 red capsicums, sliced into
    5 mm rounds
1 red onion, sliced into 5 mm
    rounds
½ teaspoon coconut sugar

EPIC GUACAMOLE

2 avocados
¼ red onion, finely diced
2 tablespoons finely chopped
    coriander leaves
1 tablespoon extra-virgin olive oil
1 teaspoon apple cider vinegar
1 long red chilli, deseeded and
    finely chopped
1 garlic clove, crushed
finely grated zest and juice
    of 1 lime
½ teaspoon sea salt

TO SERVE

Luke's Tortillas (see page 163)
coriander leaves
lime cheeks

SERVES 4

Place the chicken thighs between two sheets of baking paper and, using a meat mallet, pound to an even 1.5 cm thickness (this will ensure the chicken cooks evenly).

Place the garlic, lime zest and juice, chilli powder, cumin, coriander, oregano, paprika, 1 teaspoon of salt and half the olive oil in a large bowl and mix well. Add the chicken and use your hands to massage the marinade into the chicken until evenly coated. Cover and place in the fridge to marinate for a minimum of 1 hour or up to 6 hours.

Heat the remaining oil in a large frying pan over medium–high heat. Add the capsicum, onion, sugar and ¼ teaspoon of salt and cook for 8–10 minutes, stirring occasionally, until the vegetables start to brown. Add a splash of water and stir well, scraping any browned bits from the bottom of the pan. Cook for a further 4–5 minutes, until the capsicum is lovely and tender. Remove from the heat and set aside.

For the epic guacamole, use a fork to roughly mash the avocados in a bowl, leaving it slightly chunky at this point. Add the remaining ingredients and mix until you reach your desired level of smoothness. I like a chunky guac, so I don't mash the avo completely.

Preheat the barbecue grill to medium–hot and lightly grease the grill.

Place the chicken on the grill and cook for 2–3 minutes on each side or until golden brown and cooked through. Transfer to a wooden board, cover loosely with foil and allow to rest for a few minutes.

Once rested, cut the chicken into 1.5 cm slices and arrange on a large platter with the capsicum and onion. Serve with the epic guac, tortillas, coriander leaves and lime cheeks.

This really is a deliciously zesty take on fragrant Thai chicken. Packed as it is with so much plant goodness, you'll be adding this green satay to everything you cook in no time.

SPICY THAI CHICKEN
with GREEN SATAY

½ cup Thai basil leaves, roughly chopped, plus extra leaves to serve

⅓ cup coriander leaves, roughly chopped

1 tablespoon finely grated ginger

2 garlic cloves, crushed

1 long red chilli, finely diced

2 tablespoons tamari or coconut aminos

1 tablespoon sugar-free fish sauce

2 tablespoons olive oil

2 tablespoons coconut sugar

600 g boneless chicken thighs, skin off

2 tablespoons peanuts, toasted and roughly chopped, to serve

lime wedges, to serve

GREEN SATAY

1 avocado

1 cup coriander leaves

1 green chilli, deseeded and chopped

2 garlic cloves

finely grated zest and juice of 2 limes

250 ml (1 cup) olive oil

1 teaspoon sea salt

160 g (1 cup) peanuts, toasted

SERVES 4

For the green satay, place all the ingredients except the peanuts in a food processor and blitz to combine. Add the peanuts and pulse until mostly smooth but still a little bit chunky. Transfer to a bowl and place in the fridge until you're ready to serve.

Combine the Thai basil, coriander, ginger, garlic, chilli, tamari or coconut aminos, fish sauce, olive oil and coconut sugar in a large bowl. Add the chicken and toss to coat evenly. Cover and place in the fridge to marinate for at least 1 hour or up to 3 hours for best results.

Preheat the barbecue grill to medium.

Grill the chicken for 6–8 minutes on each side, until golden brown and cooked through. Transfer to a wooden board, cover loosely with foil and leave to rest for 5 minutes.

To serve, roughly chop the chicken and place it on a large platter. Drizzle over the green satay and sprinkle with the toasted peanuts and some extra Thai basil leaves. Serve with lime wedges for squeezing over.

I call this a cheat's schnitty because it doesn't require the usual shallow-frying method that most schnitzel recipes suggest! This crumbing mixture really crisps up nicely and I just love the char lines that come from using the barbecue grill.

CHEAT'S SCHNITTY *and* SLAW

2 x 300 g chicken breasts,
    halved widthways
100 g (1 cup) almond meal
60 g (½ cup) arrowroot flour
1 teaspoon chilli powder
1 teaspoon sea salt
125 ml (½ cup) extra-virgin
    olive oil
lime wedges, to serve

RED CABBAGE SLAW

juice of 1½ limes
2 teaspoons honey, maple syrup
    or monk fruit syrup
1 garlic clove, crushed
½ teaspoon ground cumin
½ teaspoon smoked paprika
3 tablespoons extra-virgin
    olive or avocado oil
sea salt and freshly ground
    black pepper
½ red cabbage, finely shredded
    using a mandoline

SERVES 4

For the red cabbage slaw, combine the lime juice, sweetener of choice, garlic, cumin and paprika in a mixing bowl. Slowly add the oil as you whisk the dressing and season well with salt and pepper. Add the cabbage and set aside for 15–20 minutes to allow the cabbage to absorb the flavours and soften slightly.

Preheat the barbecue grill to medium–hot.

Place the chicken breast pieces on a chopping board and pound each of them to 1–1.5 cm thickness. They don't have to be perfectly even in thickness, but make sure they aren't any thicker than 1.5 cm so they cook all the way through.

Lay out two shallow bowls and a tray for holding the raw, crumbed chicken. Place the almond meal, arrowroot flour, chilli powder and salt in one bowl and mix. Pour the olive oil into the other bowl.

Dip a chicken breast piece into the olive oil to coat it all over. Lift it out and let most of the oil drip off until you have a fairly thin coat. Move the chicken to the crumbing mixture and press it in so it sticks well, then lay the crumbed chicken on the tray. Repeat with the remaining pieces.

Grill the chicken for 6–8 minutes, turning once halfway through, until cooked through and golden brown on the outside with lovely char lines. Season well and serve with the red cabbage slaw and some lime wedges.

If there is one dish that I have to order whenever I'm eating Indian it is tandoori chicken, and I *always* ask for it to be extra hot. I've added a little more spice to this one so you can see what it is like with some extra kick, though hold back on the chilli powder if you like it milder.

TANDOORI CHICKEN *and* CUCUMBER SALAD

4 large skinless, bone-in chicken
   thighs (about 600 g in total)
sea salt and freshly ground
   black pepper
lime halves, to serve

TANDOORI MARINADE

150 g unsweetened coconut
   yoghurt
3 tablespoons extra-virgin
   olive oil
finely grated zest and juice
   of 2 limes
4 cm piece of ginger, grated
4 garlic cloves, crushed
2 teaspoons dried chilli flakes
1 teaspoon ground cumin
1 teaspoon garam masala
½ teaspoon sweet paprika
1 teaspoon sea salt

CUCUMBER SALAD

3 tablespoons extra-virgin
   olive or avocado oil
juice of 1½ limes
1 garlic clove, crushed
3 tablespoons roughly torn
   coriander leaves
½ teaspoon each of sea salt and
   freshly ground black pepper
4 Lebanese cucumbers, finely
   sliced into discs

SERVES 4

For the cucumber salad, place the oil, lime juice, garlic, coriander, salt and pepper in a bowl and whisk to combine. Add the cucumber and gently toss to coat, then place in the fridge until ready to serve.

To make the tandoori marinade, place all the ingredients in a food processor and blitz until smooth. Transfer to a large bowl.

To prepare the chicken, slice each thigh two or three times down to the bone at the thickest parts. This will help the marinade to permeate the chicken and will make the end result even tastier.

Place the chicken in the marinade and use your hands to massage it in evenly. Cover and place in the fridge to marinate for at least 30 minutes or up to 4 hours.

When ready to cook, preheat the barbecue grill to medium–hot.

Place the chicken on the grill, close the lid and cook for 20–25 minutes, turning occasionally, until charred on the outside and cooked through.

Season well with salt and pepper and serve with the cucumber salad and lime halves for squeezing over.

Nothing compares to grilled chicken wings. They cook up really fast and the skin gets so crispy with this delicious spice rub. Whenever I make these, I can't stop myself from eating nearly all of them myself, and I'm sure you won't be able to either.

SMOKY TEXAN WINGS

3 tablespoons extra-virgin olive oil
finely grated zest and juice of 2 lemons
2 teaspoons sea salt, plus extra to serve
2 teaspoons dried chilli flakes
1 teaspoon garlic powder
1 teaspoon onion powder
1 teaspoon smoked paprika
½ teaspoon cayenne pepper
½ teaspoon freshly ground black pepper, plus extra to serve
1 kg chicken wings
Chilli Aioli (see page 124), to serve

SERVES 4

Place the olive oil, lemon zest and juice, salt, chilli flakes, garlic and onion powders, paprika, cayenne and pepper in a large bowl and mix well. Add the chicken wings and use your hands to coat the chicken evenly with the marinade.

Preheat the barbecue grill to medium.

Place the wings on the grill and cook, turning and basting with the remaining marinade occasionally, for 18–20 minutes or until golden brown and cooked through.

Season the wings well with some more salt and pepper and serve with the chilli aioli for dipping.

Nothing beats a whole chook and this cooking method brings so much flavour and tenderness to the meat. Grilling the whole bird on the flames gives it a lovely smoky char that is just perfect with this finger lickin' drizzle.

FINGER LICKIN' GRILLED WHOLE CHICKEN

1 x 1.8–2 kg chicken
3 tablespoons olive oil
juice of 1½ lemons
4 garlic cloves, crushed
3 tablespoons chopped flat-leaf
    parsley leaves
sea salt and freshly ground
    black pepper

FINGER LICKIN' DRIZZLE

2 garlic cloves, crushed
2 teaspoons sea salt
finely grated zest and juice
    of 2 lemons
125 ml (½ cup) extra-virgin
    olive oil

SPICY HERB SAUCE

½ bunch of flat-leaf parsley
½ bunch of coriander
1 long red chilli, finely diced
250 ml (1 cup) extra-virgin
    olive oil
finely grated zest and juice
    of 1 lemon

CHARRED LEMON HALVES

2 lemons, halved
2 teaspoons extra-virgin olive oil

SERVES 4–6

Place the chicken in a large ziplock bag. Place the olive oil, lemon juice, garlic, parsley, 1 teaspoon of salt and ½ teaspoon of pepper in a bowl and mix well. Pour the marinade into the bag with the chicken then seal it, pressing out any air. Use your hands to massage the marinade into the chicken, making sure it is well coated. Place in the fridge to marinate, turning occasionally, for at least 1 hour or overnight for best results. (You can also do this in a large airtight container.)

For the finger lickin' drizzle, smash the garlic and salt using a mortar and pestle until a paste forms. Stir through the lemon zest and juice and olive oil. Transfer to a bowl and set aside until ready to serve.

For the herb sauce, place all the ingredients in a food processor or use a stick blender to blitz until you have a thick, chunky sauce. Cover and place in the fridge until ready to serve.

When ready to cook, prepare the barbecue for indirect cooking (see page 17), preheating one side to medium and leaving the other side completely off.

Remove the chicken from the marinade and season well with salt and pepper. Tie the legs together with string and place the chicken, breast-side down, on the side of the barbecue that is off. Close the lid and cook for 45 minutes. Flip the chicken, close the lid and cook for a further 35–40 minutes or until the juices from the leg run clear. Transfer to a wooden board, loosely cover with foil and leave to rest for 10–15 minutes.

While the chicken is resting, prepare the charred lemon halves. Coat the cut sides of the lemon with the olive oil and place, cut-side down, on the hottest part of the grill. Cook for 4 minutes or until the lemons have softened slightly and you can see lovely char lines.

Transfer the chicken to a platter, spoon over some spicy herb sauce and finger lickin' drizzle and serve with the charred lemon halves.

The size and shape of chicken tenderloins allow for really easy cooking. They won't dry out like the breast can sometimes do, and this Middle Eastern marinade really brings these tender, juicy pieces to life.

FLAME-GRILLED MIDDLE EASTERN CHICKEN

800 g chicken tenderloins
lemon wedges, to serve

MIDDLE EASTERN MARINADE

2 tablespoons ground cumin
2 tablespoons ground coriander
8 garlic cloves, crushed
2 teaspoons sea salt
3 tablespoons extra-virgin
   olive oil
½ teaspoon cayenne pepper
2 teaspoons ground turmeric
1 teaspoon ground ginger
1 teaspoon freshly ground
   black pepper
2 teaspoons ground allspice

ISRAELI SALAD

2 Lebanese cucumbers, diced
2 roma tomatoes, deseeded
   and diced
1 bunch of flat-leaf parsley,
   leaves picked and finely
   chopped
½ red onion, finely chopped
3 tablespoons extra-virgin
   olive or avocado oil
1 tablespoon apple cider vinegar
finely grated zest and juice
   of 2 limes
sea salt and freshly ground
   black pepper

SERVES 4

To make the Middle Eastern marinade, place all the ingredients in a large bowl and mix well. Add the chicken and mix with your hands to coat evenly. Cover and place in the fridge to marinate for at least 30 minutes or up to 3 hours.

For the Israeli salad, place all the ingredients in a bowl, season with salt and pepper and mix well.

Preheat the barbecue grill to medium–hot.

Place the chicken on the grill, close the lid and cook for 4–5 minutes on each side or until cooked through and golden with nice grill marks. Transfer to a wooden board, loosely cover with foil and leave to rest for 5 minutes.

Serve the chicken on a platter, topped with the Israeli salad and with lemon wedges for squeezing over.

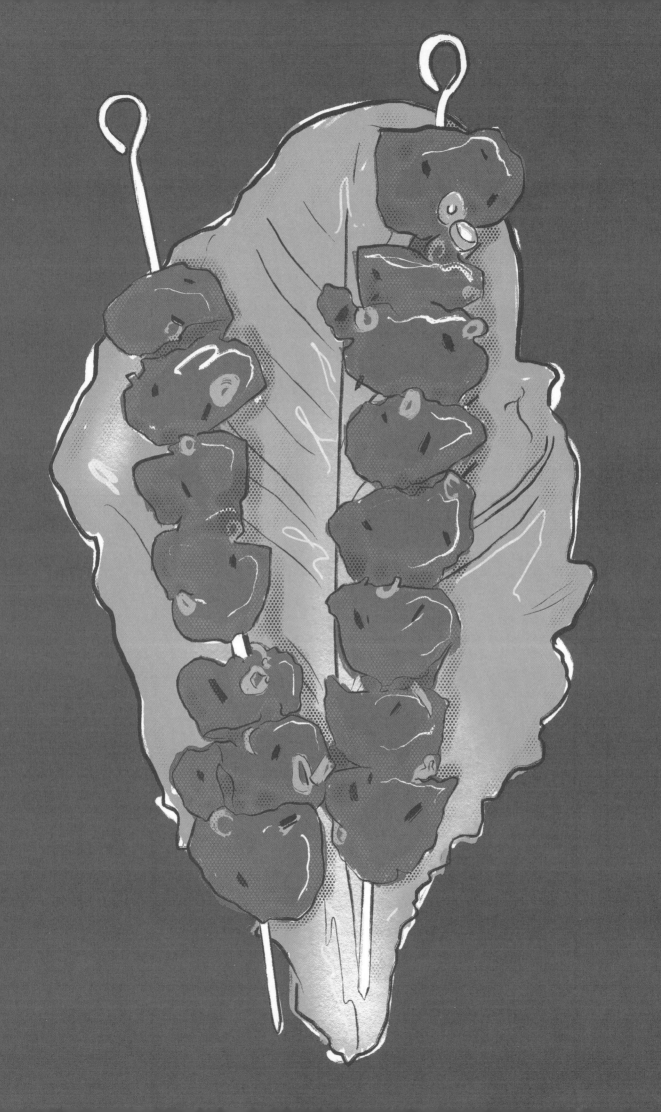

Perfect

PORK

This recipe is the ultimate indulgence when it comes to burgers! They are delicious served alongside one of my salads, such as the gorgeous green salad (see page 183) or magnificent mango salad (see page 208), but I love them just as much with my burger buns, like this. Simply add some green leaves and you're good to go!

DELUXE BACON BURGERS

6 rindless bacon rashers

2 tablespoons extra-virgin
   olive oil

1 onion, finely diced

1 carrot, grated

1 zucchini, grated

2 garlic cloves, crushed

500 g pork mince

2 tablespoons finely chopped
   flat-leaf parsley leaves

1 egg

¼ teaspoon sea salt

¼ teaspoon freshly ground
   black pepper

TO SERVE

8 Barbecue Burger Buns
   (see page 211)

1 handful of rocket leaves

125 ml (½ cup) Smoky Barbecue
   Sauce (see page 164)

SERVES 4

Preheat the barbecue flat plate and grill to medium–hot.

Place the bacon on the flat plate and cook for 4–5 minutes, turning halfway through, until softened and the fats are released. Remove the bacon from the heat and set aside to cool slightly, then roughly chop.

Add the olive oil to the flat plate with the onion, carrot, zucchini and garlic and cook for 4–5 minutes or until the onion and garlic have softened and the vegetables are slightly cooked. Remove from the heat and add to the bacon you've set aside.

In a large bowl, combine the pork mince, parsley, egg, salt and pepper. Add the cooked bacon and vegetables, then use your hands to mix everything well. Shape the mixture into eight patties.

Place the patties on the grill and cook for 3–4 minutes on each side or until golden brown on the outside and cooked through to your liking. Transfer to a wooden board, cover loosely with foil and leave to rest for 5 minutes.

Serve in burger buns with some rocket leaves and barbecue sauce.

Nothing sums up the simplicity and deliciousness of traditional Thai food like this epic combination of grilled meat, vibrant herbs, zesty lime juice and spicy dressing. This will no doubt go on serious repeat in your household.

PHUKET PORK

600 g pork neck or scotch steaks

2 tablespoons extra-virgin olive oil

½ red cabbage, cut into 4 wedges

2 shallots, finely sliced

1 bunch of mint, leaves picked

1 bunch of coriander, leaves picked

3 tablespoons finely sliced spring onion

2 tablespoons peanuts, toasted

THAI MARINADE

1 tablespoon sugar-free fish sauce

1 tablespoon coconut aminos

1 teaspoon coconut sugar

½ teaspoon freshly ground black pepper

SPICY DRESSING

3 tablespoons sugar-free fish sauce

2 teaspoons coconut sugar

2 teaspoons dried chilli flakes

finely grated zest and juice of 2 limes

SERVES 4

Use a mallet or rolling pin to lightly pound the pork steaks to about 1 cm thick. (You can always ask your butcher to do this for you.)

To make the marinade, mix the ingredients in a large bowl until the coconut sugar has dissolved. Add the pork steaks to the bowl and use your hands to coat well. Set aside at room temperature for 10 minutes.

Preheat the barbecue grill to medium–hot and brush the grill lightly with 1 tablespoon of the olive oil.

Place the marinated pork on the grill and cook for 6–8 minutes, turning halfway through, until charred on the outside and just cooked through. Transfer to a wooden board, cover loosely with foil and leave to rest for 5 minutes.

Increase the barbecue grill to hot.

While the pork is resting, brush the red cabbage pieces with the remaining olive oil and grill for 3–4 minutes on each side or until slightly softened and charred on the outside.

For the spicy dressing, place all the ingredients in a small bowl and whisk well to combine.

Once rested, slice the pork into thin strips and transfer to a bowl with the shallot. Add the dressing and toss well to combine, then add the mint, coriander and spring onion and toss again.

Scatter over the peanuts and serve with the charred red cabbage.

I love spicy food, and if you haven't noticed already, I add lots of fresh and dried chilli to my recipes. You don't always have to use the amount I recommend, or any at all for that matter, I just think it brings so much flavour to each dish. These sausages also go really well with my salsa verde salad (see page 190) if you are looking for some freshness to contrast with the spice.

SPICY PORK SAUSAGES
with CHILLI AIOLI

600 g fatty pork mince
1 teaspoon tomato paste
1 teaspoon dried chilli flakes
½ teaspoon cayenne pepper
1 teaspoon ground cumin
1 teaspoon ground coriander
2 garlic cloves, crushed
1 teaspoon dried parsley
½ teaspoon sea salt
1 red onion, thickly sliced
Charred Lemon Halves
   (see page 114), to serve
rosemary sprigs, to serve

CHILLI AIOLI

4 egg yolks
2 teaspoons dijon mustard
2 tablespoons apple cider
   vinegar
juice of 1 lime
3 garlic cloves, crushed
sea salt
400 ml extra-virgin olive or
   avocado oil, plus extra
   if needed
¼ teaspoon chilli powder,
   plus extra if needed
freshly ground black pepper

SERVES 4

For the chilli aioli, place the egg yolks, mustard, vinegar, lime juice, garlic and a big pinch of salt in a large bowl. Whiz together using a hand-held blender. With the hand-held blender still going, add the oil in a thin, even stream until all the oil has been incorporated and the aioli is thick and creamy. Stir through the chilli powder (add extra if you like things spicy), then season to taste with salt and pepper. Transfer to a serving bowl, cover and refrigerate until needed.

Place the mince, tomato paste, chilli flakes, cayenne pepper, cumin, coriander, garlic, parsley and salt in a bowl and use your hands to mix well. Cover and place in the fridge for at least 2 hours or overnight for best results.

When it's time to cook, preheat the barbecue grill to medium.

Using your hands, form the pork mixture into eight fat, evenly-sized sausages. Place the sausages on the grill and cook for 8–10 minutes, turning every few minutes, until golden brown and charred on the outside and cooked through.

Place the red onion on the grill and cook for 2–3 minutes on each side or until nicely charred.

Serve your snags with the chilli aioli, red onion, charred lemon and some sprigs of rosemary.

Any leftover chilli aioli will keep in an airtight container in the fridge for up to 1 week. It's delicious served with all kinds of skewers, sausages and grilled veggies.

Pork and pineapple make a perfect match for grilled skewers and just scream summer barbecue. The sticky glaze here cuts through the richness of the pork and sweetness of the pineapple, and will be sure to have you coming back for seconds.

STICKY PINEAPPLE *and* PORK SKEWERS

700 g pork shoulder, cut into
   4 cm pieces
sea salt and freshly ground
   black pepper
1 tablespoons extra-virgin
   olive oil
400 g pineapple, cut into
   4 cm pieces
1 red onion, cut into 4 cm pieces
12 large wooden skewers, soaked
   in cold water for at least
   20 minutes before using
2 limes, halved
1 handful of coriander leaves,
   to serve

STICKY PORK MARINADE

125 ml (½ cup) coconut aminos
125 ml (½ cup) pineapple juice
2 tablespoons coconut sugar
2 garlic cloves, crushed
1 tablespoon tamari
1 tablespoon apple cider vinegar
1 teaspoon smoked paprika
1 teaspoon ground allspice

SERVES 4

For the sticky pork marinade, combine all the ingredients in a large bowl.

Add the pork to the marinade, season with salt and pepper and toss well to coat. Cover and place in the fridge for at least 2 hours or overnight for best results.

When ready to cook, preheat the barbecue grill to medium–hot and lightly grease with the oil.

Alternately thread the pork, pineapple and onion pieces onto the prepared skewers, being mindful not to squeeze too much onto each skewer to allow proper cooking (the ingredients should only be lightly touching each other).

Grill the skewers for 6–7 minutes, turning and basting with the marinade every now and then, until golden brown and caramelised on the outside and cooked through to your liking. Transfer to a wooden board, cover loosely with foil and leave to rest for 5 minutes.

While the skewers are resting, increase the barbecue grill to hot.

Place the lime halves, cut-side down, on the grill and char for 1–2 minutes on each side or until caramelised with lovely char lines.

Divide the skewers among plates, scatter over the coriander and serve with the charred lime.

It is believed that larb is originally from Laos, but most people know it from Thai cuisine as it appears on the menus of Thai restaurants around the world. It can be made with a variety of different types of mince – pork, fish, chicken, duck and beef all work really well – so feel free to mix it up.

PORK LARB LETTUCE CUPS

2 tablespoons extra-virgin olive oil

500 g pork mince

juice of 1½ limes

2 tablespoons sugar-free fish sauce

1 long red chilli, finely chopped

2 red shallots, finely chopped

4 spring onions, green part only, finely sliced, plus extra to serve

1 handful of coriander leaves

1 handful of mint leaves

1 small handful of Thai basil leaves

1 tablespoon sesame seeds, toasted

1 tablespoon peanuts, toasted and finely chopped

1 iceberg lettuce, leaves separated

SERVES 4

Preheat the barbecue flat plate to hot and grease with the olive oil.

Place the pork mince on the flat plate and cook, using a metal spatula to break up the chunks, for 4–5 minutes or until lightly browned and crumbly. Add the lime juice, fish sauce, chilli, shallot and spring onion and use the spatula to toss everything lightly for 1 minute or so, then transfer the mixture to a large bowl. Add half the fresh herbs, sesame seeds and peanuts and toss gently to combine.

When ready to eat, take the bowl to the table, sprinkle over the remaining sesame seeds and peanuts, scatter over the remaining herbs and serve with the lettuce leaf cups for scooping up the mixture.

I have always loved the combination of pork and fruit – they go so well together. Here the salsa balances out the heat of the marinade and the saltiness of the pork.

JERK PORK *with* PINE–APPLE SALSA

2 x 400 g pork tenderloins
extra-virgin olive oil, for greasing
sea salt and freshly ground
   black pepper

JERK MARINADE

3 tablespoons extra-virgin
   olive oil
2 spring onions, green part only,
   thickly sliced
2 garlic cloves, crushed
2 bird's eye chillies, deseeded
1 tablespoon tamari or
   coconut aminos
finely grated zest and juice
   of 1 lime
1 tablespoon coconut sugar
2 teaspoons ground allspice
1 teaspoon thyme leaves
¼ teaspoon grated nutmeg
2.5 cm piece of ginger, chopped

PINE–APPLE SALSA

½ red onion, finely chopped
finely grated zest and juice
   of 1 lime
½ large pineapple, diced
2 tablespoons pineapple juice
2 granny smith apples, peeled,
   cored and cut into 5 mm dice
3 tablespoons finely chopped
   coriander leaves
1 tablespoon coconut sugar
1 long red chilli, deseeded and
   finely diced
1 spring onion, green part only,
   finely sliced

SERVES 4

To make the jerk marinade, place all the ingredients in a blender and blitz to a smooth puree.

Pour the marinade into a ziplock bag and add the pork tenderloins, turning to coat well. Seal the bag, pressing out the air, and refrigerate for 4–8 hours (the longer you leave it, the better it will be).

When ready to cook, preheat the barbecue grill to medium–low and lightly grease it with some olive oil.

Remove the pork from the marinade, allowing any excess liquid to run off, and season generously with salt and pepper.

Grill the pork, turning occasionally, for 15–20 minutes or until golden brown on the outside and cooked through to your liking. Transfer the pork to a chopping board, cover loosely with foil and leave to rest for 10 minutes.

While the pork is resting, make the salsa. Place all the ingredients in a bowl and toss well to combine.

Once rested, cut the pork into thick slices with a sharp knife. Divide the meat among plates and serve topped with the pine–apple salsa.

This recipe is my way of bringing a little bit of Nando's into your house! Portuguese cuisine really celebrates spice rubs and sauces, and here are two of my favourites.

PORTUGUESE PORK CHOPS
with PERI PERI SAUCE

100 ml extra-virgin olive oil

3 tablespoons apple cider vinegar

½ savoy cabbage, finely shredded

1 handful of flat-leaf parsley leaves, finely chopped

4 x 300 g pork chops, bone in

sea salt and freshly ground black pepper

PORTUGUESE SPICE RUB

3 tablespoons sweet paprika

1 teaspoon freshly ground black pepper

1 teaspoon chilli powder

1 teaspoon ground cumin

1 teaspoon ground cinnamon

1 teaspoon ground allspice

½ teaspoon ground nutmeg

½ teaspoon dried oregano

¼ teaspoon ground ginger

PERI PERI SAUCE

4 garlic cloves

4 bird's eye chillies

2 tablespoons lemon juice

1 tablespoon red wine or apple cider vinegar

3 tablespoons extra-virgin olive oil

½ red onion

2 teaspoons paprika

1 teaspoon dried oregano

½ teaspoon chilli powder

sea salt and freshly ground black pepper

SERVES 4

For the Portuguese spice rub, combine all the ingredients in a small bowl. Set aside until ready to use.

For the peri peri sauce, place all the ingredients in a food processor or blender and blitz until the chillies have completely broken down. Season well with salt and pepper and set aside.

Whisk 3 tablespoons of the olive oil and the vinegar in a large bowl, then add the shredded cabbage and parsley and toss well. Set aside to soften before serving.

Preheat the barbecue grill to medium.

Coat the pork chops with the remaining olive oil and season with 2 tablespoons of the Portuguese spice rub and some salt and pepper.

Place the chops on the grill and cook for 4 minutes on each side or until cooked through. Transfer to a wooden board, cover loosely with foil and leave to rest for 2 minutes.

Serve the pork with the shredded cabbage salad and peri peri sauce.

Any leftover spice rub can be stored in an airtight container or jar in the pantry for up to 1 month. Use it to rub over chicken, lamb or even veg before popping on the grill.

The key to a juicy, tender and flavoursome pork belly is in the cooking process. The secret? Low and slow, which is why barbecuing a pork belly really is a fantastic technique. Plus, because you've cooked it on the grill, you end up with an added depth of flavour, with all that smoky goodness you can only get from outdoor cooking! The more time you give the spice rub to permeate the meat, the better result you'll get when it hits the table.

CRISPY PORK BELLY with APPLE SAUCE

1 x 1 kg pork belly
Salsa Verde Salad, to serve
(see page 190)

PORK BELLY SPICE RUB

2 tablespoons sea salt
2 tablespoons coconut sugar
2 tablespoons sweet paprika
1 tablespoon garlic powder
1 tablespoon chilli powder
1 tablespoon ground cumin
2 teaspoons freshly ground
black pepper
2 teaspoons mustard powder
½ teaspoon cayenne pepper

EASY APPLE SAUCE

1.2 kg granny smith apples,
peeled, cored and sliced
6 tablespoons honey, maple
syrup or monk fruit syrup
finely grated zest and juice
of 1 lemon
40 g unsalted butter
pinch of sea salt
½ teaspoon ground cinnamon
pinch of freshly grated nutmeg

SERVES 6–8

For the pork belly spice rub, place all the ingredients in a small bowl and mix well to combine.

Using a sharp knife, score the skin of the pork belly in a criss-cross pattern. Rub with 2–3 tablespoons of the spice rub and refrigerate for at least 1 hour or up to 24 hours for best results. (The extra spice rub will keep in an airtight container for ages and works well with other cuts of meat, too.)

Preheat the oven to 220°C.

To make the apple sauce, combine the apple, sweetener of choice, lemon zest and juice, butter, salt and 3 tablespoons of water in a baking dish. Bake for 30 minutes or until the apples are very soft. Transfer the apple mixture to a food processor, add the cinnamon and nutmeg and blitz to a lovely, sauce-like consistency. Set aside.

When ready to cook, prepare the barbecue for indirect cooking (see page 17), preheating one side to medium and leaving the other side turned to low or completely off.

Place the pork belly, skin-side down, on the coolest part of the barbecue, close the lid and leave it to crisp for 20–30 minutes. Keep an eye on it throughout in case the skin begins to burn.

Once the skin is golden, puffy and crisp, turn the pork over and close the lid. Continue to cook for 1½–2 hours or until the meat is juicy and tender and can be easily pulled apart with a fork.

Once cooked, transfer to a wooden board, cover loosely with foil and leave to rest for at least 30 minutes before serving.

Slice the pork belly into thick chunks and serve with the apple sauce and my salsa verde salad.

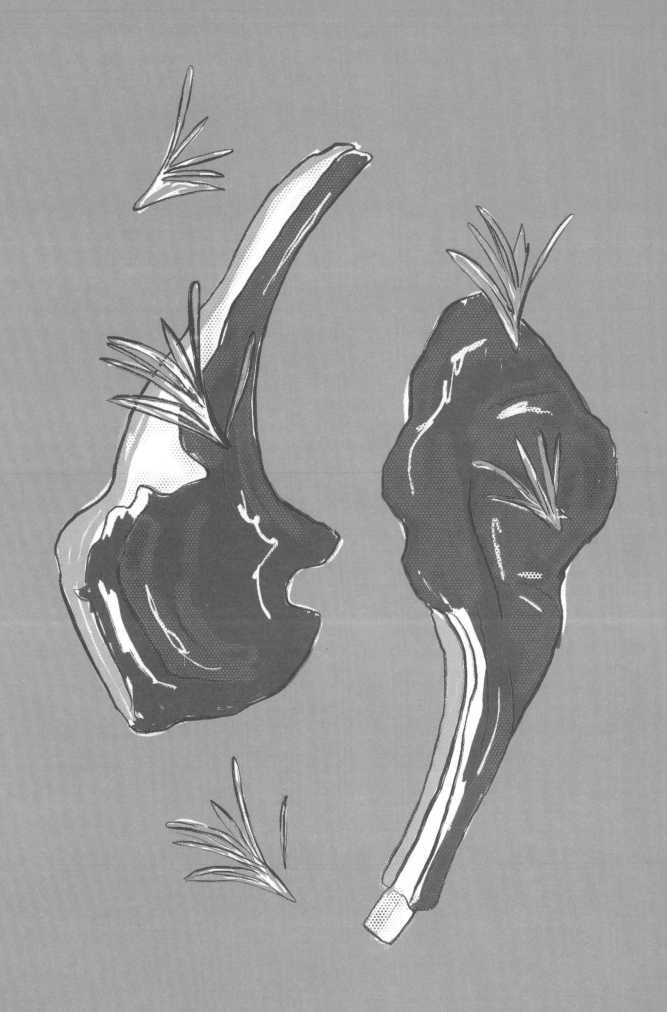

Lovely
LAMB

Rissoles are so iconically Australian they're up there with Vegemite and Tim Tams. These simple lamb rissoles are packed with veg and are especially delicious when teamed with this fresh and zingy salsa.

LOVELY LAMB RISSOLES *with* APPLE *and* MINT SALSA

2 tablespoons extra-virgin
   olive oil, plus extra for drizzling
1 red onion, finely chopped
1 carrot, grated
1 zucchini, grated
800 g lamb mince
2 tablespoons coconut aminos
1 heaped tablespoon flat-leaf
   parsley leaves
50 g (½ cup) almond meal
1 egg
sea salt and freshly ground
   black pepper
100 g baby rocket leaves
lime cheeks, to serve

APPLE AND MINT SALSA

1 granny smith apple, unpeeled,
   cored and finely chopped
3 tablespoons finely shredded
   mint leaves
finely grated zest and juice
   of 1 lemon
1 tablespoon extra-virgin
   olive or avocado oil

SERVES 4

Preheat the barbecue grill and flat plate to medium–hot. Grease the flat plate with 1 tablespoon of the olive oil.

Place the onion, carrot and zucchini on the flat plate and cook for 4–5 minutes, using a metal spatula to keep it all moving, until everything softens and becomes caramelised. Transfer to a large bowl and set aside to cool.

Once cool enough to touch, add the lamb mince, coconut aminos, parsley, almond meal and egg and season well with salt and pepper. Using your hands, mix until well combined, then shape into twelve even-sized rissoles.

Brush the grill with the remaining olive oil and cook the rissoles for 4–5 minutes on each side or until golden brown and cooked through. Transfer to a wooden board and cover loosely with foil to keep warm.

For the salsa, toss all the ingredients in a bowl to combine.

Place the rissoles on a platter and top with the apple and mint salsa and rocket leaves. Drizzle over a little more olive oil, season well with salt and pepper and serve with some lime cheeks.

Kofta are simple meatballs made from minced meat and spices, and they are popular all over the Middle East. These lamb kofta are so easy to make and are really elevated by the coconut dipping sauce.

LAMB KOFTA *with* SPICED COCONUT SAUCE

700 g lamb mince

4 garlic cloves, crushed

2 teaspoons ground cumin

2 teaspoons dried oregano

2 teaspoons sweet paprika

1 teaspoon dried chilli flakes

2 teaspoons coconut aminos, plus extra to serve

sea salt and freshly ground black pepper

8 metal skewers

2 tablespoons extra-virgin olive oil

1 handful of mint leaves, roughly torn

lemon wedges, to serve

SPICED COCONUT SAUCE

250 g (1 cup) unsweetened coconut yoghurt

½ teaspoon ground cumin

½ teaspoon sweet paprika

¼ teaspoon cayenne pepper

finely grated zest and juice of 1 lemon

sea salt and freshly ground black pepper

2 tablespoons coconut aminos

2 tablespoons extra-virgin olive oil, for drizzling

SERVES 4

For the kofta, combine the lamb mince, garlic, cumin, oregano, paprika, chilli flakes and coconut aminos in a bowl. Season generously with salt and pepper and mix thoroughly with your hands.

Divide the lamb mixture into eight evenly sized portions, then shape each portion around a skewer. Place the skewers on a tray, cover and refrigerate for 30 minutes to firm up.

Preheat the barbecue flat plate to medium and brush with the olive oil.

Cook the skewers for 2–3 minutes on each side, turning four times, or until golden brown and charred on the outside and cooked through.

To make the spiced coconut sauce, combine the coconut yoghurt, spices, lemon zest and juice in a bowl and season well with salt and pepper. Spoon into a serving bowl, drizzle over the coconut aminos and olive oil, and give it a swirl to partially combine.

Arrange the kofta on a platter, scatter over the mint leaves and serve with the spiced coconut sauce and lemon wedges on the side.

The word baharat simply means 'spice' in Arabic. Originating in the Middle East, it is commonly used in Lebanese, Syrian and Palestinian dishes. Although you can buy pre-made versions, the good news is that it's very easy to whip up your own and, in my opinion, it is way more flavourful. Here I've used baharat to coat some lamb backstraps, which are served with a fresh cucumber salsa to lighten things up.

BAHARAT BACKSTRAPS

4 x 200 g lamb backstraps, trimmed and pounded to flatten slightly

2 tablespoons extra-virgin olive oil, plus extra for brushing

sea salt and freshly ground black pepper

BAHARAT SPICE MIX

3 teaspoons smoked paprika

2 teaspoons ground coriander

2 teaspoons ground cumin

½ teaspoon ground nutmeg

½ teaspoon ground cinnamon

½ teaspoon freshly ground black pepper

¼ teaspoon ground cloves

CUCUMBER SALSA

3 tablespoons extra-virgin olive or avocado oil

finely grated zest and juice of 1 lemon

1 teaspoon dijon mustard

1 teaspoon sea salt

1 teaspoon garlic powder

½ teaspoon freshly ground black pepper

½ teaspoon dried chilli flakes

2 cucumbers, finely sliced

2 tablespoons finely chopped dill fronds

2 tablespoons finely chopped flat-leaf parsley leaves

1 tablespoon finely chopped mint leaves

SERVES 4

For the baharat spice mix, mix all the ingredients in a small bowl.

Place the lamb, spice mix and oil in a large bowl. Season well with salt and pepper and toss to coat. Set aside at room temperature for 10 minutes for the flavours to develop.

Preheat the barbecue grill to hot and brush it with a little olive oil.

Cook the lamb with the lid closed for 3–4 minutes on each side for medium–rare or until cooked to your liking. It should be golden brown and charred on the outside and soft pink in the middle. Transfer to a wooden board, cover loosely with foil and leave to rest for 5 minutes.

For the cucumber salsa, place the oil, lemon zest and juice, mustard, salt, garlic powder, pepper and chilli flakes in a large bowl and whisk well to combine. Add the cucumber and fresh herbs and toss to coat. Season with extra salt and pepper to taste.

Cut the lamb into thick slices, divide among plates and serve with the cucumber salsa.

Make a big batch of this baharat spice mix, as it is an awesome seasoning, spice rub or marinade for a wide range of proteins and veggies, and a great addition to soups and salads. Leftovers can be stored in a jar in the pantry for up to 3 months. I love adding a sprinkle to my scrambled eggs or smashed avocado with some dukkah.

I am here to announce that lamb cutlets do not need cutlery! I love how you can top these cutlets with a minty salsa, pick them up like a spoon and suck all the goodness off the bone.

LEMONY LAMB CUTLETS
with MINTY SALSA

12 lamb cutlets, French-trimmed
sea salt and freshly ground
   black pepper
extra-virgin olive oil, for brushing
1 handful of mint leaves, to serve
lemon wedges, to serve

LEMONY MARINADE

1 large handful of flat-leaf
   parsley leaves
4 rosemary sprigs, leaves picked
4 garlic cloves
100 g unsalted butter, melted
1 long red chilli, finely diced
finely grated zest and juice
   of 2 lemons

MINTY SALSA

1 bunch of mint, leaves picked
   and finely chopped
1 small garlic clove, crushed
¼ red onion, finely chopped
finely grated zest and juice
   of 1 lemon
2 tablespoons apple cider
   vinegar
125 ml (½ cup) extra-virgin
   olive or avocado oil
sea salt and freshly ground
   black pepper

SERVES 4

To make the marinade, place all the ingredients in a food processor and process to a coarse paste.

Rub the lamb all over with the marinade, season well with salt and pepper and refrigerate for 30 minutes to 2 hours (the longer you marinate it for, the more flavoursome it will be). Bring the lamb to room temperature before cooking.

For the minty salsa, mix all the ingredients in a bowl. Season with salt and pepper and set aside.

Preheat the barbecue grill to hot, then reduce the heat to medium and brush it lightly with some olive oil.

Cook the cutlets for 2–3 minutes on each side for medium–rare or until golden brown on the outside and cooked to your liking. Transfer to a wooden board, cover loosely with foil and leave to rest for 5 minutes.

Arrange the cutlets on a platter, spoon over the minty salsa and scatter over the mint leaves. Serve with some lemon wedges.

Souvlaki is a Greek dish of seasoned grilled meat that is served with tzatziki and flatbreads. The key to a juicy souvlaki is the cut of protein, such as this leg of lamb.

SIMPLE LAMB SOUVLAKI

1 x 700 g boneless lamb leg,
   trimmed of most of the fat
   and cut into 2.5 cm chunks
extra-virgin olive oil, for brushing
8 wooden skewers, soaked
   in cold water for at least
   20 minutes before using
Charred Lemon Halves
   (see page 114), to serve
Luke's Flatbreads (page 150),
   to serve (optional)

TZATZIKI

1 Lebanese cucumber, grated
180 g (¾ cup) unsweetened
   coconut yoghurt
1 tablespoon extra-virgin olive oil
1 tablespoon finely chopped
   mint leaves
1 teaspoon finely chopped
   dill fronds
1 garlic clove, finely grated
finely grated zest and juice
   of 1 lemon
sea salt and freshly ground
   black pepper

SOUVLAKI MARINADE

3 tablespoons extra-virgin
   olive oil, plus extra for brushing
1 tablespoon apple cider vinegar
finely grated zest and juice
   of 1 lemon
2 garlic cloves, crushed
2 teaspoons dried oregano
1 teaspoon dried thyme
1 teaspoon dried rosemary
1 teaspoon smoked paprika
½ teaspoon dried chilli flakes
sea salt and freshly ground
   black pepper

SERVES 4

For the marinade, mix all the ingredients in a large bowl. Season with salt and pepper to taste, then add the lamb to the bowl and toss until well coated. Cover and place in the fridge to marinate for 1–2 hours.

To make the tzatziki, place all the ingredients in a bowl, season generously with salt and pepper and mix well. Place in the fridge until ready to serve.

When ready to cook, preheat the barbecue grill to medium–hot and brush it with a little olive oil.

Thread the marinated lamb onto the prepared skewers, about four pieces per skewer, and season with salt and pepper. Place the skewers on the grill and cook for 8–10 minutes, turning every few minutes, or until golden brown on the outside and cooked through to your liking.

Arrange the skewers on a platter and serve with the tzatziki, charred lemon and flatbreads, if you like.

From Indonesia to Iran, so many cultures around the world celebrate grilled marinated meats and, whatever their name, they form a key part of many cuisines. What I love is that each country has its own unique flavour combinations and preparation techniques. The recipe below is for classic Turkish meat kebabs, with a marinade that includes tomato paste and a mix of spices for an intense flavour.

LAMB SHISH

1 x 700 g boneless lamb leg, trimmed of most of the fat and cut into 2.5 cm chunks

extra-virgin olive oil, for brushing and drizzling

12 wooden skewers, soaked in cold water for at least 20 minutes before using

24 truss cherry tomatoes

1 red onion, finely sliced

lemon cheeks, to serve

TURKISH MARINADE

4 garlic cloves, crushed

3 tablespoons extra-virgin olive oil

1 tablespoon tomato paste

½ teaspoon paprika

½ teaspoon cayenne pepper

¼ teaspoon ground cinnamon

¼ teaspoon ground cumin

2 tablespoons thyme leaves

sea salt and freshly ground black pepper

LUKE'S FLATBREADS

100 g (1 cup) almond meal

125 g (1 cup) arrowroot or tapioca flour

125 ml (½ cup) coconut milk

½ teaspoon sea salt

3–4 tablespoons coconut oil

SERVES 4

For the Turkish marinade, mix all the ingredients in a large bowl. Season to taste with salt and pepper.

Add the lamb to the marinade and toss well to combine. Cover and place in the fridge to marinate for at least 1 hour or overnight for best results.

To make the flatbreads, place the almond meal, arrowroot or tapioca flour, coconut milk, salt and 125 ml (½ cup) of water in a bowl and mix well to form a smooth, thin batter. (The more watery the batter, the thinner and crispier the flatbreads will be, so add a splash or two more if you like.)

Melt 1 tablespoon of the coconut oil in a small non-stick frying pan over medium heat. Ladle one-quarter of the batter into the pan, tilting and swirling it to coat the base in an even layer, and cook for 2–3 minutes, then carefully turn over with a spatula and cook for a further 2 minutes or until golden and cooked through. Lift the flatbread from the pan and set aside, wrapped in a clean tea towel to keep warm. Repeat with the remaining mixture, greasing the pan with a little more coconut oil in between flatbreads to make sure they don't stick to the pan.

Preheat the barbecue grill to medium–hot and brush it with a little oil.

Thread the lamb onto eight of the prepared skewers and the tomatoes onto the remaining four. Grill for about 3–4 minutes on each side or until the tomatoes are charred and blistered and the lamb is golden brown and caramelised.

To serve, slip the meat and tomatoes off the skewers and onto the flatbreads. Top with the red onion, squeeze over some lemon juice, drizzle with a little olive oil and serve immediately.

Homemade sausages are just the best! They are packed with only nourishing ingredients, plus they're super versatile. Feel free to experiment with different herbs and spices to suit your taste, or try using chicken, pork or beef mince instead of lamb.

HARISSA SNAGS *with* DICED TOMATO SALAD

600 g lean lamb mince
1 tablespoon harissa paste
1 teaspoon tomato paste
1 teaspoon ground cumin
1 teaspoon ground coriander
½ teaspoon hot chilli powder
2 garlic cloves, crushed
1 teaspoon dried mint
½ teaspoon sea salt
extra-virgin olive oil, for
    brushing

DICED TOMATO SALAD

3 tablespoons extra-virgin
    olive or avocado oil
1 tablespoon apple cider vinegar
½ red onion, finely diced
4 large tomatoes, cored and
    finely diced
1 red capsicum, deseeded and
    finely diced
1 long red chilli, finely diced
sea salt and freshly ground
    black pepper

SERVES 4

To make the snags, place all the ingredients except the olive oil in a bowl and use your hands to mix well. Cover and place in the fridge for at least 2 hours or overnight for best results.

For the diced tomato salad, pour the oil and vinegar into a large bowl and whisk well. Add the onion, tomato, capsicum and chilli to the bowl and toss with the dressing until evenly coated. Season with salt and pepper and set aside for 30 minutes to allow the flavours to develop.

When it's time to cook, preheat the barbecue grill to medium and brush it with a little oil.

Use your hands to form the lamb mixture into eight even-sized snag shapes and cook for 8–10 minutes, turning every few minutes, until golden brown and charred on the outside and cooked through.

Serve your snags topped with the diced tomato salad.

Patience is a virtue when it comes to marinating! I know it can be hard, I hear you, I always want to crack into the fun of cooking. But if you want really deep and developed flavours, give your marinades time to permeate the meat. When it comes to this lamb shoulder, marinating overnight really does yield the best results.

CHERMOULA LAMB SHOULDER *with* TAHINI SAUCE

1 x 1 kg butterflied boneless
  lamb shoulder
extra-virgin olive oil, for brushing
sea salt and freshly ground
  black pepper
1 handful of coriander leaves

CHERMOULA SPICE RUB

1 bunch of coriander, chopped
1 bunch of flat-leaf parsley,
  chopped
3 cm piece of ginger, grated
4 garlic cloves, crushed
½ onion, chopped
2 teaspoons smoked paprika
1–2 teaspoons dried chilli flakes
1 teaspoon ground cumin
1 teaspoon ground coriander
1 teaspoon sea salt
finely grated zest and juice
  of 1 lemon
125 ml (½ cup) extra-virgin
  olive oil

TAHINI SAUCE

150 g unsweetened coconut
  yoghurt
finely grated zest and juice
  of 1 lemon
2 tablespoons hulled tahini
1 tablespoon apple cider vinegar
1 garlic clove, crushed
½ teaspoon ground cumin
¼ teaspoon chilli powder

SERVES 6–8

For the chermoula spice rub, place all the ingredients in a food processor and blitz until well combined. Rub all over the lamb shoulder, cover and refrigerate for 2 hours or overnight for unforgettable results.

Remove the lamb from the fridge about 1 hour before you intend to start cooking.

Preheat the barbecue grill to medium–hot and brush it with a little oil.

Place the lamb on the barbecue, skin-side down, and brown for 15 minutes on one side, then turn and cook for a further 10 minutes. Reduce the heat to medium, close the lid and cook for a further 15–20 minutes, until charred and crispy on the outside and cooked through. Transfer to a wooden board, cover loosely with foil and leave to rest for 15 minutes.

For the tahini sauce, mix all the ingredients in a small bowl.

Slice the lamb and season well with salt and pepper. Drizzle with the tahini sauce and some olive oil, then scatter over the coriander leaves and serve.

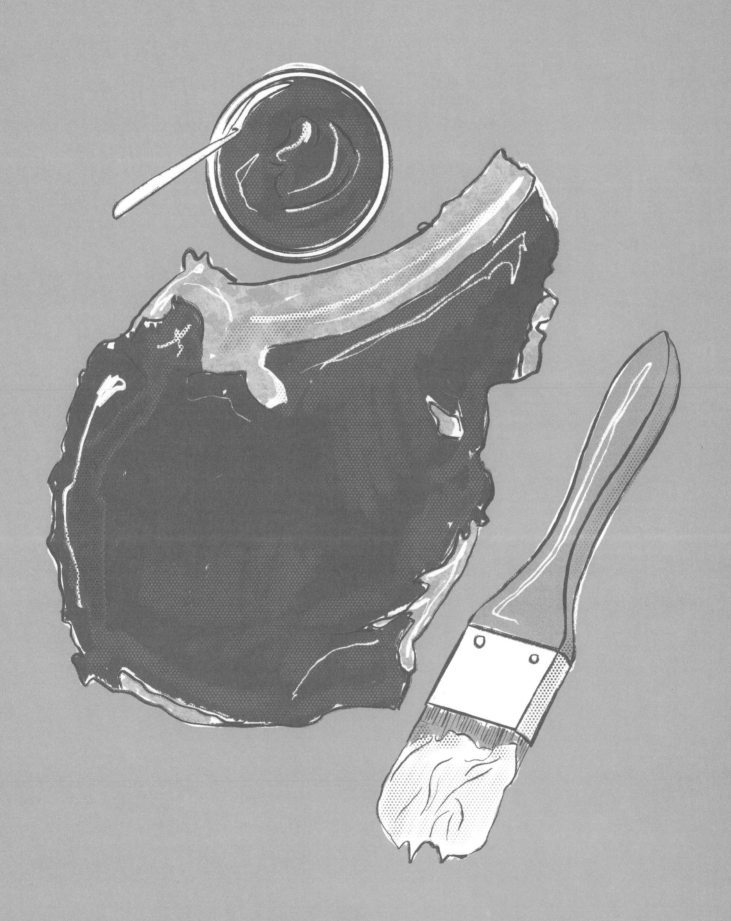

Brilliant BEEF

You can't go past a massive meaty burger stacked up high with the lot! This recipe is a flavour explosion and works just as well as a bun-less burger wrapped in lettuce leaves if you wish.

BEEF BURGER *with* THE LOT

800 g fatty beef mince
1 red onion, finely diced
2 garlic cloves, crushed
1 teaspoon dried chilli flakes
½ bunch of flat-leaf parsley,
 leaves picked and finely
 chopped
1½ tablespoons sugar-free hot
 sauce or tomato sauce
1½ tablespoons coconut aminos
2 egg yolks
sea salt and freshly ground
 black pepper
extra-virgin olive oil, for brushing

TO SERVE

8 streaky bacon strips
4 pineapple slices
4 good melting cheese slices
 (such as cheddar)
4 Barbecue Burger Buns
 (see page 211)
2 tablespoons Aioli (see page 83)
2 baby cos lettuce, leaves
 separated
1 large tomato, sliced
8 cooked beetroot slices

SERVES 4

To make the patties, place the mince, onion, garlic, chilli flakes, parsley, hot sauce or tomato sauce, coconut aminos and egg yolks in a large bowl. Season well with salt and pepper and knead with your hands so that everything is combined.

Divide the mixture into four even portions, then roll each one into a large ball and shape into a burger patty (they should be big and chunky!). Place on a plate, cover and leave to chill in the fridge for at least 1 hour.

When ready to cook, prepare the barbecue for indirect cooking (see page 17), preheating the grill to hot and leaving the other side completely off. Brush the grill with a little olive oil.

Place the patties on the grill and leave for 2–3 minutes until the edges start to colour and caramelise, then slide a metal spatula under the patties and turn them over. Cook for another 2–3 minutes, then turn again. Transfer to the cooler side of the barbecue, close the lid and cook for about 10 minutes for medium and 15 minutes for well done.

Meanwhile, grill the bacon and pineapple for about 2–3 minutes on each side or until the bacon is cooked and the pineapple is charred. Top the patties with the cheese and leave on the barbecue to melt slightly. Split the buns and warm them over the barbecue, too, if you like.

To serve, spread some aioli on the burger bun bases and top with the lettuce, tomato, pineapple, cheesy patties, beetroot and bacon. Spread some more aioli on the burger bun lids, place on top and devour!

The eye fillet is one of the most tender pieces of steak you can find. I use it for skewers as it doesn't require a long marinating time to tenderise before cooking, meaning you can throw recipes using eye fillet on the barbecue with ease and get a tender result every time.

STICKY BEEF SKEWERS
and SLAW

800 g eye fillet steak, cut into 4 cm cubes

8 bamboo skewers, soaked in cold water for at least 20 minutes before using

3 tablespoons extra-virgin olive oil

sea salt and freshly ground black pepper

STICKY BEEF SAUCE

250 ml (1 cup) Smoky Barbecue Sauce (see page 164)

3 tablespoons maple syrup

2 garlic cloves, crushed

2 teaspoons ground cumin

2 teaspoons ground coriander

1 teaspoon dried chilli flakes

EASY ICEBERG SLAW

½ iceberg lettuce, finely shredded

2 celery stalks, cut into matchsticks

2 green apples, cored and cut into matchsticks

½ carrot, cut into matchsticks

½ red onion, finely sliced

125 g (½ cup) Aioli (see page 83)

SERVES 4

Preheat the barbecue grill to medium–hot.

While your barbecue comes up to heat, make the sticky beef sauce. Place all the ingredients in a saucepan over medium heat (use your side burner if your barbecue has one) and cook, stirring occasionally, for 6–8 minutes or until thickened. Transfer to a bowl and set aside.

Thread the beef onto the prepared skewers, drizzle with the olive oil and season with salt and pepper. Place on the grill and cook for 2–3 minutes on each of the four sides or until charred and caramelised on the outside and cooked through to your liking. Transfer to a wooden board, cover loosely with foil and leave to rest for 5 minutes.

To make the easy iceberg slaw, combine the lettuce, celery, apple, carrot and red onion in a bowl, add the aioli and gently toss together.

Place the skewers on a platter, spoon over some sticky beef sauce and serve with the slaw and remaining sauce on the side.

Marinating the beef in lime juice not only adds incredible flavour to this Mexican-inspired dish, it also helps make the meat extra mouth-wateringly tender. Love the taste of this spice rub? Use it on any of your favourite cuts of meat to add some spice and zest!

CHILLI-LIME BEEF TACOS

600 g skirt steak
finely grated zest and juice
   of 3 limes, plus extra wedges
   to serve
3 tablespoons extra-virgin
   olive oil
½ red onion, finely diced
1 avocado, diced
1 tomato, deseeded and diced
1 handful of coriander leaves

CHILLI AND CUMIN SPICE RUB

2 teaspoons sea salt
1 teaspoon dried chilli flakes
1 teaspoon coconut sugar
1 teaspoon ground cumin
½ teaspoon ground coriander
½ teaspoon smoked paprika
½ teaspoon garlic powder
½ teaspoon onion powder
½ teaspoon freshly ground
   black pepper

LUKE'S TORTILLAS

2 large eggs, beaten
250 ml (1 cup) coconut milk
125 g (1 cup) arrowroot or
   tapioca flour
3 tablespoons coconut flour
½ teaspoon sea salt
2–3 tablespoons extra-virgin
   olive oil, coconut oil or butter

SERVES 4

Place the steak in a bowl, pour over the lime juice and leave to marinate for 30 minutes at room temperature.

To make the tortillas, whisk all the ingredients except the oil or butter in a bowl to form a smooth batter. Heat a little of the oil or butter in a frying pan over medium heat. Pour 60 ml (¼ cup) of the mixture into the pan, then tilt and swirl the pan to spread the batter into a 10 cm circle. Reduce the heat to low and cook for 1–2 minutes until sturdy enough to flip, then cook for 1–2 minutes on the other side until cooked through, puffed up and golden brown. Transfer the tortilla to a plate and repeat this process, adding a little more oil each time, to make eight small tortillas. (You can also make four large tortillas, if you prefer.)

Meanwhile, to make the spice rub, combine all the ingredients and the lime zest in a small bowl. Coat both sides of the steak with the spice rub, using your fingers to press firmly to ensure that the rub sticks to the meat.

Preheat the barbecue grill to hot and grease with a little of the olive oil.

Place the steak on the grill and cook for about 5 minutes on each side. Transfer to a wooden board, cover loosely with foil and leave to rest for 10 minutes. Once rested, cut the steak into thin strips.

Place the red onion, avocado, tomato and remaining oil in a bowl and mix well.

Top the tortillas with the avocado mixture and steak, scatter over the coriander leaves and serve with some lime wedges.

My preferred method for making these tortillas is with a really good non-stick frying pan, but if you like, you can also cook them on the flat plate of your barbecue. Just make sure you use a generous amount of oil to prevent them from sticking.

Owing to their large size and the fact that they contain meat from two of the most prized cuts of beef, T-bones are generally considered one of the highest quality steaks. Cooking the meat on the bone with all the delicious fat around the cut makes for a great eating experience, especially when partnered with this barbecue sauce – it's so simple to make and is bursting with the most beautiful flavours.

TERRIFIC T-BONES
with MUSTARD and
BARBECUE SAUCE

4 x 400 g T-bone steaks
2 tablespoons extra-virgin
   olive oil, plus extra for brushing
sea salt and freshly ground
   black pepper
100 g baby rocket leaves
wholegrain mustard, to serve

SMOKY BARBECUE SAUCE

70 g (½ cup) coconut sugar
1 red onion, finely diced
3 tomatoes, finely diced
2 garlic cloves, crushed
2 tablespoons balsamic vinegar
1 tablespoon tomato paste
½ teaspoon cayenne pepper
sea salt and freshly ground
   black pepper

SERVES 4

To make the smoky barbecue sauce, place a saucepan over medium–high heat (use your side burner if your barbecue has one). Add the coconut sugar and cook, stirring with a wooden spoon, for 3–4 minutes or until it begins to caramelise. Add the onion, tomato, garlic, vinegar, tomato paste and cayenne pepper, reduce the heat to medium–low and simmer, stirring occasionally, for 15 minutes or until the onion has completely softened and the sauce has begun to thicken. Season with salt and pepper to taste, transfer to a bowl and set aside until ready to serve.

Preheat the barbecue grill to medium–hot.

Brush the steaks with a little olive oil and season well with salt and pepper. Place on the grill and cook for 5 minutes on each side for medium–rare or until cooked to your liking. Transfer to a wooden board, loosely cover with foil and leave to rest for 5 minutes.

Once rested, transfer the steaks to serving plates and add the rocket. Drizzle the remaining olive oil over the rocket and serve with generous helpings of smoky barbecue sauce and mustard.

Make a big batch of this smoky barbecue sauce so that you can have it on hand to serve with my Texan wings (see page 110) or bacon burgers (see page 120). It will keep in an airtight container or jar in the fridge for up to 1 week.

Another super-tender, prized cut of meat, these rib-eyes are slathered in a delicious Cafe de Paris butter for eye-popping flavour. This butter first originated in the 1940s at the Cafe de Paris in Switzerland and today there are many variations, but the core ingredients are mixed herbs, capers, worcestershire sauce and cayenne.

RIDICULOUSLY GOOD RIB-EYE

2 x 400–500 g rib-eye steaks, on the bone
1 tablespoon extra-virgin olive oil
sea salt and freshly ground black pepper

CAFE DE PARIS BUTTER

125 g unsalted butter, softened
1 shallot, finely diced
1 garlic clove, finely diced
2 teaspoons wholegrain mustard
1 tablespoon chopped chives
2 tablespoons chopped flat-leaf parsley leaves
2 tablespoons baby capers, rinsed and drained
2 anchovies in oil, drained
1 teaspoon cayenne pepper
finely grated zest and juice of ½ lemon

HOMEMADE WORCESTERSHIRE SAUCE

2 tablespoons dijon mustard
250 ml (1 cup) coconut aminos
2 tablespoons coconut sugar
2 tablespoons apple cider vinegar
2 teaspoons garlic powder
2 teaspoons onion powder
1 teaspoon ground cinnamon
1 teaspoon sea salt
1 teaspoon freshly ground black pepper

SERVES 4

To make the worcestershire sauce, place all the ingredients in a large bowl and whisk until well combined.

For the Cafe de Paris butter, place all the ingredients and 2 teaspoons of the worcestershire sauce in a food processor and blitz until smooth. Transfer to a piece of baking paper, shape into a log, roll up and twist the ends to seal. Chill for about 30 minutes or until firm, then cut into 5 mm thick slices.

When ready to cook, preheat the barbecue grill to hot.

Drizzle the steaks with the olive oil and season well with salt and pepper. Place on the grill and cook for 6 minutes on each side or until cooked to your liking. Transfer the steaks to a tray or roasting tin, cover loosely with foil and leave to rest for 10 minutes.

Once rested, cut the beef away from the bone and slice thickly. Top with rounds of Cafe de Paris butter (it will melt into a delicious, oozy mess) and serve with a crisp salad, such as my gorgeous green salad (see page 183) or salsa verde salad (see page 190).

This homemade worcestershire sauce is not only incredibly tasty but also nutritious. Leftovers can be stored in an airtight container or jar in the fridge for up to 1 month.

BRILLIANT BEEF

Beef fillets are a great tender cut of meat, making them perfect for quick cooking as skewers. This recipe takes that wonderful pairing of rosemary and beef to another level by using rosemary sprigs as skewers and infusing all that herby goodness into an oil that will have you licking your fingers.

LEMONY ROSEMARY SKEWERS

800 g eye fillet steak, cut into 3 cm cubes
extra-virgin olive oil, for brushing
sea salt and freshly ground black pepper

ROSEMARY OIL

2 bunches of rosemary, leaves picked, 8 long woody stems reserved
4 garlic cloves, finely chopped
1 long red chilli, finely chopped
1 teaspoon sea salt
1 teaspoon freshly ground black pepper
finely grated zest and juice of 1 lemon
125 ml (½ cup) extra-virgin olive oil

SERVES 4

For the rosemary oil, place the rosemary leaves, garlic, chilli, salt, pepper and lemon zest in a food processor and blitz to a coarse paste. Transfer to a bowl and stir through the lemon juice and oil.

Place the beef in a large bowl and pour over 3 tablespoons of the rosemary oil, reserving the rest for later. Cover and place in the fridge to marinate for at least 1 hour or overnight for best results.

When ready to cook, preheat the barbecue grill to medium–hot and brush it with a little oil.

Thread the marinated beef onto the rosemary sprigs as skewers, then place on the grill and cook for 10–12 minutes, turning every 2–3 minutes, for medium–rare or until cooked through to your liking. Transfer to a wooden board, cover loosely with foil and leave to rest for 5 minutes.

Season the skewers well with salt and pepper, drizzle over the remaining rosemary oil and serve.

What makes the scotch fillet such a deliciously juicy and tender cut of beef is the abundant marbling of good-quality fat than runs through it. This means that scotch fillet steaks are able to be cooked really quickly, while remaining incredibly moist and flavoursome.

SENSATIONAL SCOTCH FILLET
with GREEN OLIVE TAPENADE

4 x 150 g scotch fillet steaks
olive oil, for brushing
sea salt and freshly ground
   black pepper
Gorgeous Green Salad with
   Avocado Dressing (page 183),
   to serve

GREEN OLIVE TAPENADE

120 g (1 cup) pitted green olives
1 bunch of flat-leaf parsley,
   leaves picked
1 tablespoon olive oil
1 tablespoon apple cider vinegar
finely grated zest and juice
   of 1 lemon
2 garlic cloves, crushed
3 teaspoons baby capers, rinsed
   and drained
freshly ground black pepper

SERVES 4

For the green olive tapenade, place all the ingredients in a food processor and blitz until combined but still a bit chunky. Taste and add a little extra pepper, if you like (it shouldn't need any salt).

Preheat the barbecue grill to hot.

Brush the steaks with a little olive oil and season well with salt and pepper. Place on the grill and cook for about 2 minutes on each side for medium–rare or until cooked to your liking. Transfer to a wooden board, cover loosely with foil and leave to rest for 5 minutes.

Once rested, divide the steaks among plates, top with the tapenade and serve with my gorgeous green salad.

Short ribs are lovely and tender and have a lot more flavour than some other cuts of beef because they have the bone in. When you cook short ribs, it's really hard to mess them up, and when you serve them they look great on the bone, like a restaurant meal at home.

REALLY GOOD RIBS

3 kg beef short ribs, cut into individual ribs
sea salt and freshly ground black pepper

MELT-IN-THE-MOUTH MARINADE

750 ml (3 cups) beef stock
100 g (¾ cup) coconut sugar
100 ml maple syrup
3 tablespoons apple cider vinegar
50 g dijon mustard
1 teaspoon smoked paprika
1 teaspoon dried chilli flakes
4 rosemary sprigs, leaves picked and finely chopped
2 teaspoons freshly ground black pepper

SERVES 6–8

To make the marinade, place all the ingredients in a large bowl and stir well until the coconut sugar has dissolved.

Add the ribs to the marinade and, using your hands, mix well to coat the ribs evenly. Cover and place in the fridge to marinate for a couple of hours or overnight for best results.

When ready to cook, prepare the barbecue for indirect cooking (see page 17), preheating it to 150°C with the lid closed, but leaving one side completely off.

Remove the ribs from the marinade, place them in a large barbecue-safe roasting tin and transfer to the barbecue. Pour over 250 ml (1 cup) of the marinade, season with salt and pepper and cover with foil, sealing the edges well.

Place the tin on the cooler side of the barbecue, close the lid and roast for 3½–4 hours or until the meat is very tender and falls away with a fork.

Meanwhile, pour the remaining marinade into a heavy-based saucepan over medium heat (use your side burner if your barbecue has one). Bring to a simmer, skimming off any foam, and cook for 40–45 minutes or until reduced to about 250 ml (1 cup) of thick, saucy goodness.

Once the ribs are tender and cooked to your liking, pour one-third of the reduced marinade over the beef. Place back on the barbecue and cook with the lid closed, basting every 20 minutes, for a further 1 hour or until sticky and glazed.

Pile the ribs onto a platter, drizzle over the rest of the reduced marinade and serve. These ribs go really well with my apple, beetroot and cashew slaw (see page 184).

This tender cut of beef is a little bit of luxury in every mouthful. It's the perfect main course to cook for a gathering of friends and family – a real crowd-pleasing show-stopper for the middle of the table, especially when served up with some special veggie sides.

BANGIN' BEEF FILLET

1 x 1–1.2 kg beef fillet
3 tablespoons extra-virgin
   olive oil

HERB RUB

2 teaspoons dried thyme
2 teaspoons dried chilli flakes
1½ teaspoons sea salt
1½ teaspoons freshly ground
   black pepper
finely grated zest of 1 lemon

HORSERADISH BUTTER

80 g salted butter, softened
2 garlic cloves, crushed
1 tablespoon finely grated
   horseradish
1 tablespoon finely chopped
   chives
1 tablespoon finely chopped
   flat-leaf parsley leaves
sea salt and freshly ground
   black pepper

SERVES 6–8

Start by preparing the beef fillet. If your fillet is thinner at one end, neatly fold the end under itself to form an even thickness, then tie kitchen string along the fillet at 3 cm intervals to keep it neat and cylindrical.

For the herb rub, mix all the ingredients in a small bowl.

Coat the beef in the olive oil, then rub it all over with the herb rub. Set aside at room temperature for 30 minutes.

Meanwhile, make the horseradish butter. You need the butter to be really soft for this, so if it is too firm, slightly soften it in the microwave or using a double boiler until it's almost runny but still holding its shape. Add the garlic, horseradish, chives, parsley and a generous amount of salt and pepper and mix until all the ingredients are well combined. Spoon the butter into a small bowl and set aside to firm up.

Preheat the barbecue flat plate to hot.

Place the beef fillet on the flat plate and sear for 15 minutes, turning every 3–4 minutes, or until browned and caramelised all over. Now prepare the barbecue for indirect cooking (see page 17), turning off one of the gas burners and lowering the heat elsewhere to medium.

Place the fillet on the coolest part of the barbecue, close the lid and cook, turning halfway through, until cooked to your liking. It should take about 10–15 minutes for medium–rare (the internal temperature should be 52–55°C when tested with a meat thermometer) or 25–30 minutes for medium to well done (60–65°C).

Transfer to a wooden board, cover loosely with foil and leave to rest for 5–10 minutes. Once rested, uncover the beef fillet and remove the string.

To serve, slice the meat into 2 cm thick slices, dollop over the horseradish butter and enjoy with my perfect roast potatoes with rosemary (see page 57), if you like, or some of your other favourite sides.

BRILLIANT BEEF

Gone are the days of boring snags wrapped in bland bread! These easy snags are flavoured with baharat spice and served on cauliflower hummus. What's not to love?

MIDDLE EASTERN SNAGS

1 red onion, finely sliced

finely grated zest and juice of 1 lemon

1 tablespoon apple cider vinegar

sea salt and freshly ground black pepper

8 wooden skewers, soaked in cold water for at least 20 minutes before using

1 teaspoon sumac, plus extra to serve

2 tablespoons finely chopped flat-leaf parsley leaves, plus extra leaves to serve

MIDDLE EASTERN SNAGS

500 g beef mince

½ onion, finely diced

½ teaspoon ground allspice

3 tablespoons finely chopped flat-leaf parsley leaves

1 teaspoon Baharat Spice Mix (see page 144)

1 teaspoon dried chilli flakes

2 tablespoons pine nuts, toasted, plus extra to serve

2 garlic cloves, crushed

CAULIFLOWER HUMMUS

1 large head of cauliflower, broken into small florets

3 tablespoons extra-virgin olive oil, plus extra for brushing

3 tablespoons hulled tahini

finely grated zest and juice of 1 lemon

1 garlic clove, crushed

¼ teaspoon ground cumin

¼ teaspoon ground coriander

sea salt and freshly ground black pepper

SERVES 4

Preheat the oven to 200°C and line a baking tray with baking paper.

To make the cauliflower hummus, place the cauliflower florets on the prepared tray, drizzle with 1 tablespoon of the olive oil and toss well to coat. Roast for 15–20 minutes or until cooked through and softened, then transfer to a food processor and blitz with the remaining oil, 2 tablespoons of water and all the other ingredients until smooth and creamy. Season with salt and pepper to taste and set aside.

Place the onion, lemon zest and juice and apple cider vinegar in a bowl. Season with salt and pepper and mix well. Leave to soften for 15–20 minutes.

Meanwhile, preheat the barbecue grill to hot and brush it with a little oil.

For the Middle Eastern snags, place all the ingredients in a large bowl, season well and mix to combine. Divide the mixture into eight even-sized portions and roll each into a sausage shape. Thread the meat onto the prepared skewers. Place on the barbecue, close the lid and cook for 3–4 minutes on each side or until charred on the outside, cooked through and juicy.

Spread the cauliflower hummus onto serving plates and top with the snags. Stir the sumac and parsley through the onions, then pile them over the snags. Sprinkle over a little extra sumac, then scatter over some parsley leaves and a few more pine nuts. Drizzle over a little olive oil and serve immediately.

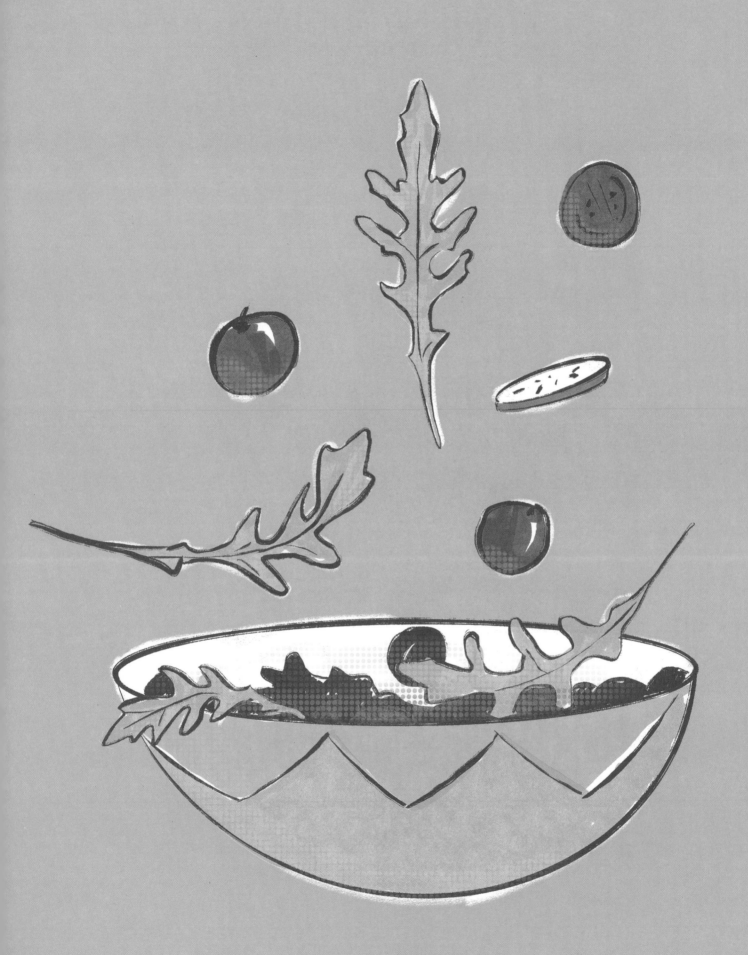

Stunning SALADS and SIDES

Never has there been a more delicious way to eat your greens. This is a really simple but slightly different take on a green salad, and the creamy avo dressing makes it the ultimate crowd pleaser. Don't be tempted to make it in advance, though – it's best prepared just before serving to prevent the avocado from oxidising over time.

GORGEOUS GREEN SALAD
with AVOCADO DRESSING

1 bunch of flat-leaf parsley, leaves picked

1 bunch of mint, leaves picked

1 bunch of dill, fronds picked

1 bunch of chervil, leaves picked

1 loosely packed cup watercress

1 loosely packed cup baby rocket leaves

1 butter lettuce, leaves separated and torn

2 tablespoons pumpkin seeds, toasted and finely chopped

AVOCADO DRESSING

125 ml (½ cup) extra-virgin olive or avocado oil

1 avocado

1 handful of coriander leaves

1 tablespoon apple cider vinegar

1 teaspoon chilli powder

finely grated zest and juice of 1 lime

pinch of sea salt

SERVES 4

For the avocado dressing, blitz all the ingredients in a food processor until smooth and creamy.

Place all the salad ingredients in a large bowl and toss to combine. Spoon over the dressing and serve immediately.

This is coleslaw, but not as you know it. Often you'll see it with shredded cabbage as the hero ingredient, but the word slaw can also simply mean a shredded or chopped salad of raw veggies, coated in a vinegar-based dressing. This slaw will look just stunning on the table at your next barbie.

GREEN APPLE, BEETROOT and CASHEW SLAW

1 loosely packed cup baby rocket leaves

1 loosely packed cup watercress

1 small handful of pea shoots

2 granny smith apples, cored, quartered and finely sliced

2 small beetroot, scrubbed and very finely sliced with a mandoline (if you have leaves, reserve them)

2 small candy beetroot, scrubbed and very finely sliced with a mandoline (if you have leaves, reserve them)

1 small bunch of marjoram, leaves picked

2 tablespoons cashews, toasted and roughly chopped

DRESSING

125 ml (½ cup) extra-virgin olive, avocado, macadamia or hemp oil

finely grated zest and juice of 1 lemon

3 tablespoons apple cider vinegar

sea salt and freshly ground black pepper

SERVES 4

For the dressing, whisk all the ingredients in a bowl until nicely emulsified.

In a large bowl, toss the rocket, watercress, pea shoots, apple, beetroot and beetroot leaves, if you have them. Add the marjoram and toss gently again, then drizzle over the dressing and scatter over the cashews. Toss once more and serve.

I first discovered chargrilled cos when eating my way around San Francisco. I loved it so much that it has now become one of my barbecue staples whenever I get the flames cranking. I hope you love it as much as I do.

CHARRED COS *with* GREEN TAHINI DRESSING

3 tablespoons extra-virgin
   olive oil
1 tablespoon chilli flakes
sea salt and freshly ground
   black pepper
4 baby cos lettuce, halved
   lengthways
3 tablespoons macadamias,
   toasted and roughly chopped
Charred Lemon Halves
   (see page 114), to serve

GREEN TAHINI DRESSING

1 avocado, mashed
3 tablespoons hulled tahini
1 garlic clove, crushed
3 tablespoons extra-virgin olive
   or avocado oil, plus extra
   if necessary
1 tablespoon apple cider vinegar
finely grated zest and juice
   of 2 lemons
sea salt and freshly ground
   black pepper

SERVES 4

For the dressing, place all the ingredients in a small bowl and mix well with a whisk or spoon. (The mixture will be quite thick and creamy, so add 1–2 tablespoons of extra oil to loosen it up to your liking if need be.) Season with salt and pepper to taste and set aside.

Preheat the barbecue grill to medium.

Place the olive oil, chilli flakes and a pinch each of salt and pepper in a bowl and whisk well.

Brush the cos halves with the olive oil mixture, then transfer, cut-side down, to the barbecue and cook for 2–3 minutes on each side or until nicely charred all over.

Transfer the charred cos to a large serving dish, dollop on the green tahini dressing and scatter over the toasted macadamias. Season well with salt and pepper and serve with the charred lemon.

I call this a cheat's salad because there are so few ingredients required you'll feel like you're cheating with how incredibly tasty and sexy this dish looks on the table. Go on, give it a try and find out for yourself.

CHEAT'S PEACH SALAD *with* SMASHED RASPBERRY DRESSING

4 yellow or white peaches, stones removed and flesh cut into wedges

1 tablespoon extra-virgin olive or avocado oil

2 loosely packed cups watercress

1 treviso radicchio, leaves separated and roughly torn

1 tablespoon baby capers, rinsed and drained

SMASHED RASPBERRY DRESSING

3 tablespoons extra-virgin olive or avocado oil

finely grated zest and juice of 1 lemon

1 small handful of chervil or flat-leaf parsley leaves, finely chopped

1 tablespoon apple cider vinegar

100 g raspberries

sea salt and freshly ground black pepper

SERVES 4

Preheat the barbecue grill to hot.

Coat the peach in the oil, then cook for 1–2 minutes on each side or until slightly softened and beautifully charred. Set aside on a plate.

In a large bowl, toss the watercress, radicchio and capers.

To make the dressing, place the oil, lemon zest and juice, fresh herbs and vinegar in a bowl or jar and either whisk or shake well. Add the raspberries and use a fork to roughly mash them. Whisk or shake well, until you've got a lovely pink dressing with some chunky raspberry pieces. Season to taste with salt and pepper.

Add the peaches to the salad, pour over the dressing and toss gently to ensure everything is well coated. Pile onto a large platter and serve.

This recipe features my take on the classic Italian green sauce, salsa verde, which is traditionally a combination of fresh green herbs, garlic and acid in the form of lemon and vinegar. I've deliberately avoided using a food processor for this gorgeous dressing to keep it chunky, authentic and fresh.

SALSA VERDE SALAD

2 baby fennel bulbs, finely shaved using a mandoline or very sharp knife

2 cups baby rocket leaves

2 granny smith apples, cored and sliced into thin discs

SALSA VERDE DRESSING

16 green olives, pitted and roughly chopped

½ cup flat-leaf parsley leaves, finely chopped

½ cup loosely packed mint leaves, roughly chopped

2 tablespoons capers, rinsed, drained and halved

1 tablespoon apple cider vinegar

finely grated zest and juice of 2 lemons

2 garlic cloves, crushed

125 ml (½ cup) extra-virgin olive or avocado oil

1 teaspoon dijon mustard

sea salt and freshly ground black pepper

SERVES 4

For the dressing, place all the ingredients in a bowl. Season well with salt and pepper and mix to combine.

In a large bowl combine the fennel, rocket and apple. Pour over the dressing, toss to coat and serve in a large bowl.

This colourful, vibrant, flavour-packed salad is incredibly refreshing and perfect for a hot summer's day! The addition of pistachio gives it just the right amount of crunch. Feel free to use whatever apples you have and play around with the fresh herbs – recipes like this are really flexible.

ZESTY APPLE *and* WATERMELON SALAD

3 golden delicious or granny smith apples, cored and cut into batons

800 g seedless watermelon, rind discarded and flesh cut into batons

finely grated zest and juice of 2 lemons

2 tablespoons apple cider vinegar

2 tablespoons extra-virgin olive or avocado oil, plus extra for drizzling

1 cup loosely packed coriander leaves

1 cup loosely packed mint leaves

3 tablespoons unsalted pistachio kernels, toasted and roughly chopped

sea salt and freshly ground black pepper

SERVES 4

Place the apple, watermelon, lemon zest and juice, vinegar, oil, coriander and mint in a large bowl. Using your hands, gently mix everything well.

Transfer the salad to a large serving platter. Scatter over the pistachios, drizzle over a little more olive oil, season well with salt and pepper and enjoy.

I just love the simplicity of this recipe and how quick and easy it is to throw together!
The golden zucchini really make this salad stand out on the table, but if you can't
find them, just using all green zucchini works really well, too.

ZUCCHINI *and* MACADAMIA SALAD

3 tablespoons extra-virgin
  olive or avocado oil
2 teaspoons wholegrain or
  dijon mustard
finely grated zest and juice
  of 1 lemon
sea salt and freshly ground
  black pepper
2 green zucchini, finely sliced
  into a combination of ribbons
  and rounds with a mandoline
2 golden zucchini, finely sliced
  into a combination of ribbons
  and rounds with a mandoline
1 handful of baby rocket leaves
3 tablespoons macadamias,
  toasted and roughly chopped

SERVES 4

Place the oil, mustard and lemon zest and juice in a large bowl, add salt
and pepper to taste and whisk well.

Add the zucchini and rocket and gently toss to combine.

Pile onto a large platter and sprinkle over the macadamias to finish.
Serve immediately.

STUNNING SALADS AND SIDES

Some fruit really lends itself to being grilled on the barbecue and pineapple is definitely a standout! It holds its shape well and becomes lovely and caramelised, with incredible char marks.

CHARRED PINEAPPLE SALAD

3 tablespoons coconut sugar

3 tablespoons extra-virgin
   olive oil

2 teaspoons sea salt

1 pineapple, cored and cut into
   long batons

2 celery stalks, trimmed and
   finely sliced

2 green apples, cored and finely
   sliced into rounds

2 red apples, cored and finely
   sliced into rounds

¼ white cabbage, finely
   shredded

50 g (½ cup) pecans, toasted
   and roughly chopped

flat-leaf parsley leaves, to serve

COCONUT DRESSING

125 g (½ cup) unsweetened
   coconut yoghurt

finely grated zest and juice
   of ½ lemon

2 tablespoons extra-virgin olive
   or avocado oil

1 tablespoon maple syrup

sea salt and freshly ground
   black pepper

SERVES 4

Preheat the barbecue grill to medium–hot.

Combine the coconut sugar, olive oil and salt in a large bowl and whisk well. Add the pineapple and use your hands to mix and coat evenly.

Place the pineapple on the grill and cook for 4–5 minutes on each side, until golden brown, charred and caramelised. Remove from the barbecue and allow to cool slightly.

Meanwhile, make the coconut dressing. Place all the ingredients in a bowl, season generously with salt and pepper and whisk well.

Toss the celery, apple and cabbage in a large bowl, then arrange on a platter and top with the pineapple. Scatter over the pecans, spoon on the dressing and sprinkle with a few parsley leaves.

Carpaccio is traditionally a dish of meat or fish, finely sliced and served raw. This is my plant-based take on the classic appetiser, still packed with all the flavours you know and love.

GARLICKY TOMATO CARPACCIO

2 garlic cloves, crushed

3 spring onions, very finely sliced

1 teaspoon capers, rinsed, drained and finely chopped

3 tablespoons extra-virgin olive oil, plus 1 tablespoon extra for drizzling

2 tablespoons red wine vinegar

sea salt and freshly ground black pepper

2 large heirloom tomatoes (about 400 g in total), cut into 2 mm thick slices

2 tablespoons finely chopped coriander leaves

¼ long green chilli, deseeded and finely chopped

SERVES 4

In a bowl, combine the garlic, spring onion, capers, olive oil and vinegar. Season generously with salt and pepper and mix well.

Lay the tomato slices out on a large serving platter or plates, slightly overlapping them, and season with a little salt. Spoon the garlicky salsa evenly over the top, scatter over the coriander and chilli and finish with a last drizzle of olive oil.

This is my take on the traditional Indian raita that would normally be made with yoghurt or curds. My version features cherry tomatoes and is dairy free as it contains coconut yoghurt – perfect for those with a dairy intolerance. There's also a zesty kick from the lemon and lime juice and zest.

ZESTY SUMMER RAITA

2 Lebanese cucumbers
250 g (1 cup) unsweetened
    coconut yoghurt
1 garlic clove, crushed
finely grated zest and juice
    of 1 lemon
finely grated zest and juice
    of 1 lime
½ bunch of coriander, leaves
    picked and roughly chopped
½ bunch of mint, leaves picked
    and roughly chopped
½ teaspoon garam masala,
    plus extra to serve
200 g cherry tomatoes,
    quartered

SERVES 4

First prepare your cucumbers. Finely grate one of them and gently squeeze out the liquid. Slice the other one lengthways into thin ribbons using a mandoline.

In a bowl, combine the grated cucumber, coconut yoghurt, garlic, lemon and lime juice, fresh herbs, garam masala and cherry tomatoes.

Transfer to a serving bowl and top with the cucumber ribbons, lemon and lime zest and an extra sprinkle of garam masala. Serve immediately.

The original Italian panzanella was thought to have been created as a way for peasants to use stale bread by soaking it in tomato juices and olive oil. My version swaps out the stale bread for charred barbecue burger buns, and it is crispy and delicious.

PERFECT PANZANELLA

2 Barbecue Burger Buns
    (see page 211)
extra-virgin olive oil, for drizzling
800 g mixed tomatoes, roughly
    chopped
3 tablespoons capers, rinsed
    and drained
1 small red onion, very finely
    sliced
12 anchovies in oil, drained and
    finely sliced
sea salt and freshly ground
    black pepper
2 tablespoons balsamic vinegar
3 tablespoons extra-virgin
    olive or avocado oil
1 bunch of basil, leaves picked

SERVES 4

Preheat the barbecue grill to medium–hot.

Roughly tear the burger buns into 3 cm pieces and drizzle generously with olive oil. Grill, turning occasionally, for 5–6 minutes or until all the edges are charred.

Meanwhile, combine the tomato, capers, onion and anchovy in a large bowl. Season well with salt and pepper, then add the balsamic vinegar and oil and gently toss.

Add the basil and charred burger bun pieces, season with a little more salt and pepper and toss well. Serve.

This is one of my favourite salads – the combination of chilled veggies, zingy lime tahini and nutty za'atar is just amazing.

CHILLED CHOPPED SALAD
with GREEN ZA'ATAR

3 tablespoons extra-virgin
   olive oil
finely grated zest and juice
   of 1 lemon
½ teaspoon each of sea salt and
   freshly ground black pepper
12 cherry tomatoes, chopped
1 red capsicum, deseeded
   and chopped
2 small cucumbers, chopped
4 spring onions, finely sliced on
   an angle
1 large handful of coriander
   leaves, roughly chopped

GREEN ZA'ATAR

50 g unsalted pistachio kernels,
   roughly chopped
1 teaspoon sesame seeds, toasted
1 teaspoon dried oregano
1 teaspoon thyme leaves, finely
   chopped
1 teaspoon sumac
¼ teaspoon ground cumin

LIME–TAHINI DRESSING

3 tablespoons hulled tahini
2 tablespoons extra-virgin
   olive oil
½ teaspoon each of sea salt and
   freshly ground black pepper
finely grated zest and juice
   of 1 lime
2 teaspoons apple cider vinegar
1 garlic clove, crushed

SERVES 4

Whisk the olive oil, lemon zest and juice, salt and pepper in a large bowl. Stir through the tomato, capsicum, cucumber, spring onion and coriander. Place in the fridge to chill while you make your green za'atar and lime–tahini dressing.

For the green za'atar, place all the ingredients in a small bowl and mix until combined. Set aside.

For the lime–tahini dressing, place all the ingredients in a small bowl and mix well.

To serve, divide the salad among plates, spoon over the dressing and sprinkle over the za'atar to finish.

I almost called this salad The Ultimate Aussie Salad as it celebrates some of my favourite iconic Aussie ingredients, such as mangoes and macadamias! The fresh herbs really shine when balanced by the fruit and slightly sweet dressing. This will be on repeat in your backyard!

MAGNIFICENT MANGO *and* MACADAMIA SALAD

2 mangoes, peeled and cut into thin strips
1 bunch of Thai basil, leaves picked
1 bunch of Vietnamese mint, leaves picked
1 long red chilli, finely sliced
1 pink grapefruit, peeled and cut into segments
400 g savoy cabbage, finely shredded
1 red onion, finely sliced
70 g (½ cup) macadamias, toasted and roughly chopped
1 tablespoon sesame seeds, toasted

GINGER DRESSING

3 tablespoons extra-virgin olive or avocado oil
3 tablespoons lemon or lime juice
1 tablespoon coconut aminos
1 teaspoon coconut sugar
1 teaspoon sugar-free fish sauce
2 teaspoons finely grated ginger

SERVES 4

For the dressing, mix all the ingredients in a small bowl.

Place the mango, basil, mint, chilli, grapefruit, cabbage and onion in a large bowl, add the dressing and toss well to combine.

To serve, transfer the salad to a large platter and top with the toasted macadamias and sesame seeds. Enjoy.

You'll be hard pressed to find a tastier, fluffier, crunchier or healthier burger bun than these bad boys. They're easy to prepare, toast up an absolute treat and can be enjoyed with other recipes, such as my deluxe bacon burger (see page 120) or perfect panzanella (see page 205). They are also incredibly good charred on the grill and slathered with butter or olive oil. Huge thanks to Pete Evans for this recipe – he has truly mastered the ultimate burger bun.

BARBECUE BURGER BUNS

70 g (1 cup) psyllium husk
70 g (½ cup) coconut flour
3 tablespoons flaxseeds
3 tablespoons chia seeds
3 tablespoons pumpkin seeds
3 tablespoons sunflower seeds
3 tablespoons sesame seeds
1 tablespoon coconut sugar
2½ teaspoons gluten-free
   baking powder
1½ teaspoons sea salt
1 tablespoon apple cider vinegar
3 eggs
2 tablespoons coconut oil,
   melted
almond meal or arrowroot flour,
   for dusting
butter or extra-virgin olive oil,
   to serve

MAKES 4-6

Preheat the oven to 180°C and line a baking tray with baking paper.

In a high-speed blender or food processor, combine the psyllium husk, coconut flour, flaxseeds, chia seeds, pumpkin seeds, sunflower seeds and sesame seeds and process until the seeds are finely chopped.

Transfer to a large mixing bowl, add the coconut sugar, baking powder and salt and mix well.

In a separate mixing bowl, whisk the apple cider vinegar, eggs and 450 ml of water until smooth and combined. Add this wet mixture to the dry mixture, along with the melted coconut oil. Mix everything until it forms a wet dough.

Lightly flour a board with some almond meal or arrowroot flour and knead the dough on the board for 1 minute. Divide the dough into four large or six slightly smaller portions and roll into balls.

Place on the prepared tray, 5 cm apart to leave room for spreading. Bake for 50–60 minutes, rotating the tray halfway through to ensure even cooking.

Check to see if the rolls are ready by tapping the base of one roll – if it sounds hollow, remove them from the oven. If they still sound a bit dense and heavy inside, continue cooking them a little longer.

Remove from the oven and allow to cool on the tray for 5 minutes before transferring to a wire rack to cool completely. To serve, slice in half, char on the barbecue grill and slather in butter or olive oil.

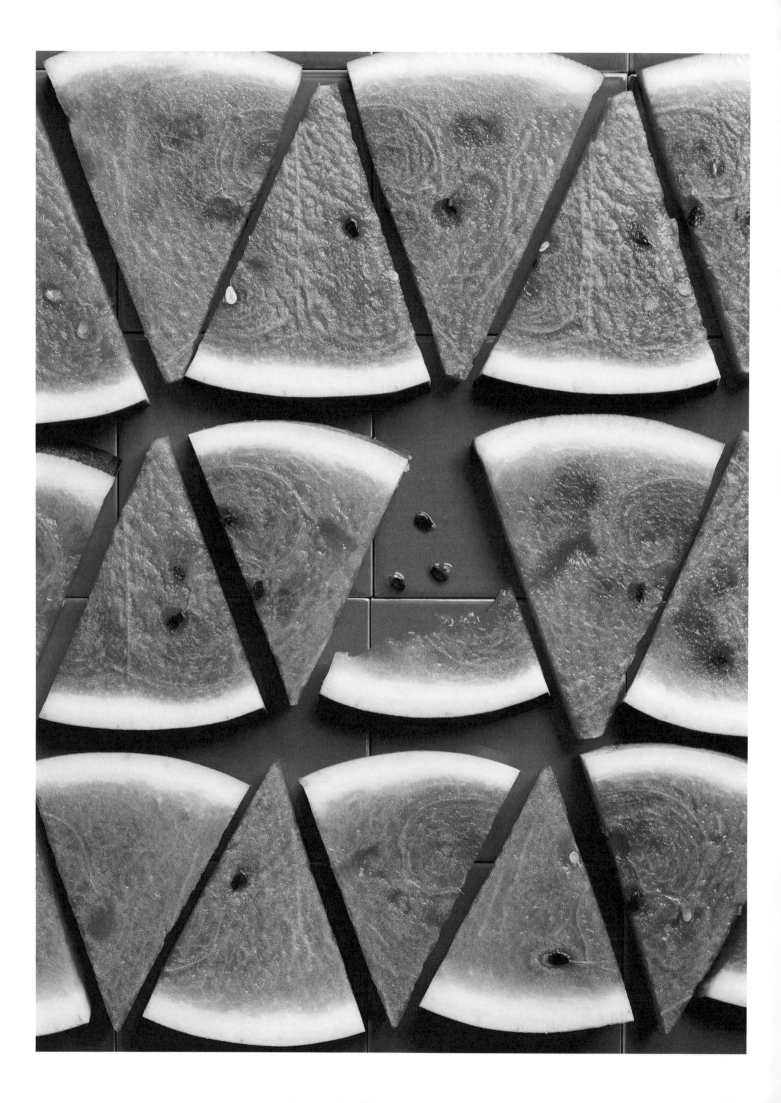

CONVERSION CHARTS

Measuring cups and spoons may vary slightly from one country to another, but the difference is generally not enough to affect a recipe. All cup and spoon measures are level.

One Australian metric measuring cup holds 250 ml (8 fl oz), one Australian metric tablespoon holds 20 ml (4 teaspoons) and one Australian metric teaspoon holds 5 ml. North America, New Zealand and the UK use a 15 ml (3-teaspoon) tablespoon.

LENGTH

METRIC	IMPERIAL
3 mm	⅛ inch
6 mm	¼ inch
1 cm	½ inch
2.5 cm	1 inch
5 cm	2 inches
18 cm	7 inches
20 cm	8 inches
23 cm	9 inches
25 cm	10 inches
30 cm	12 inches

LIQUID MEASURES

ONE AMERICAN PINT	ONE IMPERIAL PINT
500 ml (16 fl oz)	600 ml (20 fl oz)

CUP	METRIC	IMPERIAL
⅛ cup	30 ml	1 fl oz
¼ cup	60 ml	2 fl oz
⅓ cup	80 ml	2½ fl oz
½ cup	125 ml	4 fl oz
⅔ cup	160 ml	5 fl oz
¾ cup	180 ml	6 fl oz
1 cup	250 ml	8 fl oz
2 cups	500 ml	16 fl oz
2¼ cups	560 ml	20 fl oz
4 cups	1 litre	32 fl oz

DRY MEASURES

The most accurate way to measure dry ingredients is to weigh them. However, if using a cup, add the ingredient loosely to the cup and level with a knife; don't compact the ingredient unless the recipe requests 'firmly packed'.

METRIC	IMPERIAL
15 g	½ oz
30 g	1 oz
60 g	2 oz
125 g	4 oz (¼ lb)
185 g	6 oz
250 g	8 oz (½ lb)
375 g	12 oz (¾ lb)
450 g	16 oz (1 lb)
900 g	32 oz (2 lb)

OVEN TEMPERATURES

CELSIUS	FAHRENHEIT
100°C	200°F
120°C	250°F
150°C	300°F
160°C	325°F
180°C	350°F
200°C	400°F
220°C	425°F

CELSIUS	GAS MARK
110°C	¼
130°C	½
140°C	1
150°C	2
170°C	3
180°C	4
190°C	5
200°C	6
220°C	7
230°C	8
240°C	9
250°C	10

THANK YOU!

Releasing my first book in 2013 was an absolute privilege, and if you'd asked me back then if I could ever see myself releasing a 12th book in 2020, I would have told you that you're dreaming. But here we are, and I can hand on heart say it has been an incredible ride making it this far. As fortunate as I feel to experience this publishing journey, none of it would be at all possible without you my readers and the hard-working people who are actually the true heroes behind each page.

Firstly, to the Pan Macmillan and Plum family, thank you for always having my back. Mary, Jane and Ash, specifically, for making sure what we release together is timely, relevant and aesthetically beautiful. The vibrancy, colour and life on each page of this book truly represents the excitement and passion you guys have for creating incredibly stunning books in the food space. Your foresight into what Australians want to cook, combined with your expertise in what you do, has resulted in this gorgeous book we've made together.

People often ask me how on earth we create all the beautiful images of the mouth-watering food in my books. For this book, like all my previous Plum books, it was an incredible team effort. I feel so lucky to work with such a talented group of people who put their heart and soul into every part of the process, from sourcing the best ingredients, preparing them with love, styling them in a gorgeous but also approachable way and then finally capturing them with vibrancy and life that jumps off the page. So to Emma and Sarah who cooked, Deb who styled and Mark who shot, thank you for doing another book with me and bringing your A-game.

You can have the best publishing team in the industry combined with a world-class creative crew on set, but without all the pieces to the puzzle, it wouldn't be the book it is today. So to Simon for his sharp eye during the edit, Andy for his creative genius on design, and Charlotte and the publicity team for getting the book into the hands of hungry cooks everywhere – thank you.

Everyone mentioned above is crucial to making a book, but what really sets a book apart from others on the shelves is you guys, for actually picking it up and allowing me to share my passion for quick and easy recipes that are always delicious and good for you too. So thank you for continuing to support me, my books and everything I am setting out to achieve. This book is for you.

INDEX

A PLUM BOOK

First published in 2020 by
Pan Macmillan Australia Pty Limited
Level 25, 1 Market Street,
Sydney, NSW, Australia 2000

Level 3, 112 Wellington Parade,
East Melbourne, Victoria, Australia 3002

Text copyright © Luke Hines 2020
Photography Mark Roper copyright © Pan Macmillan 2020
Design Andy Warren copyright © Pan Macmillan 2020

The moral right of the author has been asserted.

Design and illustration by Andy Warren
Typesetting by Kirby Jones
Editing by Simon Davis
Index by Helena Holmgren
Photography by Mark Roper
Prop and food styling by Deb Kaloper
Food preparation by Emma Warren and Sarah Watson
Colour reproduction by Splitting Image Colour Studio
Printed and bound in China by Imago Printing International Limited

A CIP catalogue record for this book is available from the National Library of Australia.

All rights reserved. No part of this book may be reproduced or transmitted by any person or
entity (including Google, Amazon or similar organisations), in any form or means, electronic
or mechanical, including photocopying, recording, scanning or by any information storage
and retrieval system, without prior permission in writing from the publisher.

10 9 8 7 6 5 4 3 2 1